Homeward

Contemplation is the art of pondering over a thought
for a long time and reflecting deeply upon it.

The aim of contemplation is to lead from an intellectual
understanding to the Experience of the Thought.

Denis Pickwell

BALBOA
PRESS
A DIVISION OF HAY HOUSE

Balboa Press books may be ordered through booksellers or by contacting:

Balboa Press
A Division of Hay House
1663 Liberty Drive
Bloomington, IN 47403
www.balboapress.com.au
1 (877) 407-4847

Because of the dynamic nature of the Internet, any web addresses or links contained in this book may have changed since publication and may no longer be valid. The views expressed in this work are solely those of the author and do not necessarily reflect the views of the publisher, and the publisher hereby disclaims any responsibility for them.

The author of this book does not dispense medical advice or prescribe the use of any technique as a form of treatment for physical, emotional, or medical problems without the advice of a physician, either directly or indirectly. The intent of the author is only to offer information of a general nature to help you in your quest for emotional and spiritual well-being. In the event you use any of the information in this book for yourself, which is your constitutional right, the author and the publisher assume no responsibility for your actions.

Any people depicted in stock imagery provided by Thinkstock are models, and such images are being used for illustrative purposes only. Certain stock imagery © Thinkstock.

Print information available on the last page.

ISBN: 978-1-4525-2782-6 (sc)
ISBN: 978-1-4525-2783-3 (e)

Balboa Press rev. date: 03/25/2015

For

Margaret

Always there to support me;
my love,
and my lifetime companion.

Contents

Acknowledgement

Over the years I have read many books and listened to a lot of people.
They have inspired me to make changes in my life.
These authors are too numerous to mention by name
and I would probably forget some of them.
They have all contributed in some measure to
bring me to this point in my journey.
But especially, I owe much to the thoughts expressed in a book called
"A Course in Miracles" [1]
To me it is the most significant book I have ever read
and you will find some quotations from it in the
verses that follow.
In the Epilogue I have also used an extract from another exceptional book
"Dialogue on Awakening" [2]
by
Tom and Linda Carpenter.

[1] All quotes from A Course in Miracles
are from the Combined Volume, Second Edition
The Foundation for Inner Peace
P.O.Box 598
Mill Valley, CA 94942
U.S.A

[2] *Dialogue on Awakening - P250*
The Carpenter's Press
P.O.Box3437
Princeville, Hawaii 96722

Introduction

These verses; I do not call the poems though perhaps they are, were written over a number of years. They express my own experiences as I searched for the answers to all my questions.

Words are not the best method for communication but they are the best that most of us have. To try to put into words what one feels is a bit like trying to describe the flavour of an orange or how you feel as you watch a beautiful sunset. Nevertheless I found that, for me, the "poem" format of these verses was the best way I had for doing this.

These verses have two basic aspects:

1. To intellectually explain the subject
2. To provide words that will lead to the "inner experience" beyond the intellect.

You will notice there is some repetition in the thoughts expressed. This is not a mistake, because these ideas are fundamental spiritual Thoughts and repetition, of course, imprints these on our minds. So it is natural that they should appear that way in these verses.

Sometimes you will come across a saying or maybe a book and you say "Wow! That's great". Then you mention it to someone else whom you feel would be interested and they say without enthusiasm "Oh, yes, I suppose it is".

I hope you will find a "Wow" factor in these verses that will have some appeal, some "resonance" within you. If you do, then I suggest you do not hurry.

*   Take time to read. There is no rush.
*   Read whichever one appeals to you at the time.
*   Take a section and think about it.
*   Contemplate.
*   Maybe just read one at a time.
*   **Feel** the thought behind the words.

The Longer Poems:

If you start to read one of the longer verse sets by all means take your time, but do go on to the end. The longer ones have a good deal of explanation before coming to a conclusion at the end and, of course, to understand the conclusion generally means understanding how it was reached.

Conclusions:

If any of the thoughts expressed in these verses upset you or if you disagree with them; that is ok. You then have the opportunity to look closely at what disturbs you and from this can come a whole new vision. Everyone chooses their own road, but all roads lead eventually to that Living Presence and, as has been said: "From Him you cannot wander....." [1]

Strange as it may seem, I frequently re-read my own writings and am often blessed again by the thoughts that they express. I trust they will be a blessing to you also. I hope that as you read you will try to **feel** the Thought that lies behind the words and experience more deeply the **Presence** that dwells in us all.

"And turn you to the stately calm within, where in holy stillness dwells the Living God you never left, and Who did not leave you" [2]

- **Denis**

"A Course in Miracles"

[1] T13-X1-11:5
[2] T-18-1-8:2

Explanation of References

Unless otherwise indicated all references are from **"A Course in Miracles"** .

The "Course" is divided into three main parts:
The Text – referenced as "T"
The Workbook – referenced as – "W"
The Manual for Teachers – referenced as "M"
Clarification of Terms – referenced as "C"

Example 1 : T13-X1-11:5 "From Him you cannot wander and there is….."
Where -
T = Text
13= Chapter
X1=Section
11= Paragraph
5 = Sentence

Example 2: W-p1. 169.5:2 "And in His Being He encompasses all things"
Where –
W = Workbook
P1 = Part 1
169 = Lesson No. 169
5 = Paragraph 5
2 = Sentence 2

The other parts of the "Course" are annotated in a similar manner to the above but the details are not noted as there are no quotations from them in "Homeward".

Homeward

I am quiet for a moment
And my frantic mind has
Stilled its onward rush.
Distractions and the glitter
Of this world cease
To attract
For just an instant;
And I feel it yet again.

I am not always conscious of it,
Yet, like some nagging tooth
It always seems to be there.
Always, always the thought remains
A restlessness
A longing,
An inner intuition –
I am not at home.

I try to make a home
With family, and friends
Who love me.
Yet a house is not a home.
Nor is a family,
For little ones grow up
And form their own.

So we remain,
Looking for completion in
Each other;
Looking for a resting place,
A place of peace,
A garden of quiet,
A place where we belong,
A home.

And there remains
A yearning.
And when we stop to think a moment,
We feel
A deep gut-wrenching pull,
A homesickness,
A knowledge that there is
A "place"
Where we belong –
All our being leans towards it
With an inner pull
That cannot be denied.
We search for happiness,

For some contentment
In this life.
And find it not.
Always searching,
Always seeking,
Always looking
For fulfillment;
Which eludes us.

Still we look;
For what?
We know not.
Yet search we must.
And deep within us calls
The Voice
That pulls our heartstrings
With Its Love,
And calls us Home.

And so we turn
And move at last
Towards the Home
We love so well.

Some think that there is
Still another choice;
That something in this world
Will bring us all the joy we seek.
But seek it not,
For only misery
And sorrow
Lie down that road.
There is nowhere else to go
But back to Him,
Who is our Source,
Our Peace,
Our Beloved,
And our Home.

1998

A Note about

Homeward

I was only 7 when I went to boarding school in Melbourne, Australia. My parents lived in New Guinea (my father was a doctor) and there were no schools there in 1939. I knew what it was to be homesick.

I guess everyone has had that feeling at sometime. It is loneliness, a form of depression, a not wanting to do anything, dejection, a yearning. It can be acute or it can be a sort of background feeling.

And so it is with all of us who inhabit planet earth. We feel we are missing something. We team up with a partner with the expectation that our "other half" will make up that "something missing". But it does not happen.

There is within us a yearning for a home that we have somehow lost. Some do not recognise it that way; some search for such a home here but never find it; some distract themselves with pleasure or work to try to obscure or fulfil that yearning - a yearning for our real Home.

So we search – and there is the recognition that we are somehow going somewhere. We have a vague recollection of a condition, a state of being, not a place; but we were happy there – it was our home.

So this life seems to be a journey. Some say this existence is purposeless; and yet we feel that there is a destination that we must reach. This longing, this homesickness, is something deeply imbedded in each one of us. We ultimately MUST find our real home.

Nostalgia

You hear a song,
A plaintive melody,
A song you've heard before
- Or something in it anyway –
That pulls the strings upon your heart.

Nostalgia – that's what we call it.
And yet it speaks of something else.
What is nostalgia but
A sense of yearning
A longing for something that you've lost,
Something that you've known
In some past and ancient time,
Almost beyond recall.
And yet you know
It has been heard before;
And in this song,
This snatch of melody,
You hear it once again;
The recognition that somewhere,
Deep within
The inner recesses
Of your mind and spirit
Is your home.

A home you never left
But thought you had,
Where dwells
The Presence of the Living God.
He with you
And you with Him.

One in Spirit
One in Love
One in Power
Forever and forever and forever

1998

A Note about

Nostalgia

The most common thing that everyone values seems to be - their photo albums!

Why?

I remember an old lady whose husband recently died. She said "Well, at least I have some wonderful memories".

We seem to treasure our memories. Our photographs help us to remember things and remember them more vividly.

Yet what are these but memory tracks in our minds, of things we did (or didn't do), of the great times, the relationships, the family, the adventures – yet all of this exists no more.

We do not want to remember the bad times, the fear, the misery, the suffering. We want to relive the good ones. We have a longing to go back to "the good old days" yet, at the time, we do not remember them all being so good. The good parts are the only ones we want to remember.

What is nostalgia but a desire to live again those days when we were happiest; a longing for something past, or lost. Yet we never found it then and we will never find it in anything outside of us. Happiness is within. So is Heaven, the name we give to our real Home. It is this, deep down in our minds that we remember. It is this we long for. It is only here that we are truly happy and complete.

Searching

Searching

It is the nature of mankind
To search out all that he can find.
He searches in this world to see
The building blocks of all that be.
He searches too his inner soul
Because he thinks that there his goal
Will reach an end.

So search we must
But to what end?
Is it happiness we hope to find
Or Freedom
Or completion,
Satisfaction
Power or peace?

We look to money
And possession
Status
And relation.
We're told in these
We reach our goals.
Success is what we want?

But still the search goes on.
The lack of satisfaction deep within
Drives us.
Search we must
And one day, at some future time
The search will end.

Still we search, but do not find.
When will it end?
If not today, when will it be?

If it must end one day
Then one day it will be
Today.
So why not now?

What hinders you?
Your search will end
When you desire
To know the Truth
And nothing else.
When all you see or sense
You value not
And your one desire is
Simply this -
To be complete in Him.

2001

A Note about

Searching

Everybody searches. This is the reason we came into this world- to find "**it**". The problem is most people do not know what "it" is.

We search for the awareness of what we really are; to know ourselves, to know Reality.

The search will end when we deeply and sincerely want to know the truth. It was never hidden from us.

We just didn't (and maybe don't) want to know.

Why not now?

Happiness

Happiness

What is there in this world
But searching
For all the happiness that can be yours?
What else but this is here
For us to seek, but pain?

These two,
Which seem to alternate
One with the other.
For every bit of pleasure
There seems to be the pain
That follows.

Certain it is we search
For what will make us happy.
And try to fill our days
With pleasure.
Yet are we concerned
If days go by and we are still
Enjoying the pleasure that we sought.
How long can this go on?
Can we sustain the pleasure
And the happiness so long?

We are concerned;
For too much happiness
Assuredly will bring us pain!
This can't go on;
For pain and suffering
Seem far more constant
Than the fleeting pleasures
Which briefly pass our way.

Pain and pleasure follow each other,
Like night and day.
Their purpose is the same,
For they assure us that the body
Is our one reality.

On this we can depend
Our body feels the pleasures
Of the senses
Does it not?
And most certainly are we aware
Of pain.
"You are here within this body-
You can be hurt,
You can have pleasure too-
But at the cost of pain"[1]

There are different sorts
Of suffering;
Some much worse than others;
A tiny stab of pain,
A little worldly pleasure,
And yet they are a single sound-
A call for healing
And a plaintive cry for help
Within a world of misery.[2]

We seek for happiness
Within this world.
But if every pleasure
Has its corresponding pain,
Then where can happiness be found?

Is pleasure but response?
The joy of touch
And sight and sound;
Does it depend on stimulation

Of the body's nerves
Its cells and surfaces
Its response to light,
Or nearness of another body?

Or is there more to happiness than this?

Is pleasure just response
From senses,
Activated
By some outside cause?
Can the body think and know
Its course of action sure?
Or is it perhaps
Directed by the mind it serves,
And here interpreted
All the body sends it?
Thus is the mind
The experiencer of the pleasure
And the pain,
That searches desperately
For happiness.

For happiness is
Within the mind;
Not in things external
To the body.
True joy can be found
Within the spirit,
Within the mind itself
Which expresses our reality.

Search as you may
For happiness outside yourself
And it will pass away
As does a sudden zephyr
Or a cooling breeze in summer.

For pleasure cannot last
It cannot, for its source is flawed.
It cannot give you what it promises,
For all true joy must come only from
One Source;
From which comes Life Itself.
And this one Source of Joy
Still lies within us all;
And from this well
Springs up the happiness we seek.

For Love
And Joy
And Happiness
Are One,
And all are yours to keep.

Within you lies the Source,
That can be found
By all who have a little willingness
To go beyond the "pleasures" of the world
And find within, the happiness they seek.

Pain and pleasure
Pleasure, pain;
These two are both
One and the same.
They but obscure the Source
Of Happiness and Joy
Whose name is
Love.

Jan.1999

¹   T27-VI-2:2
²   T27-VI-6:5

A Note about

Happiness

I heard a little ditty many years ago:

"Happiness, happiness,
Everybody's searching for happiness.
Round and round and round they race
And everybody's searching in a different place"

Everybody is searching. They want happiness, but they don't know where to find it. Some are not even aware of what they really want.
The power of advertising and rhetoric tells us it is in success or status or sex or possessions, money or power or something else
but
The answer does not lie outside. It is within you.
This is where lasting happiness abides.

What Are Words?

It is difficult, I find,
To express my piece of mind
In prose;
In such a way
That all may understand
The words I say.

And so it is, that when I go
To rhyme;
The words I find
Just seem to fit,
And can explain ideas
Which otherwise
I'd miss.

But what are words?
Ideas expressed in sound.
And not just that;
But thoughts as well
Give rise to words
Within the mind.
It is with these we think,
And reason,
And flesh out our perceptions
Of the world around us
And within.

Communication now
With thoughts
Eludes us.
So it is that we express ourselves
In words.
A poor attempt;
One second hand

Which often fails to say
The things we feel
And great ideas which do not seem the same
Expressed in words.

The real idea was in the mind.
And it was there communicated
Loud and clear.
You understood it, even unexpressed in words
Instinctively you knew
The thought,
And what it meant.

Whence come ideas?
How can we know the truth
Of what we "hear"?
Some say 'tis but the brain
That stores the memories
And that, from these, we
Manufacture our ideas.
But others say that there are thoughts
Which go beyond the brain.
It does not have within itself
Creativity, imagination,
Or wisdom, that comes
Unbidden to the mind.

Undoubtedly the mind
Picks up the thoughts of others,
Those around us.
But there are greater Thoughts than these.
Each one of us can think
The Thoughts of God,
If he is willing
And can be still a little while.

For when the mind is stilled
Of all its frantic thoughts

And clanging words,
And wills to listen for a moment,
Then
It hears the thoughts within;
But faintly at the start
Then with increasing clarity
And lessening doubt
It understands
The **Word of God!**

And from each one who hears
The **Thoughts** go out to others
In this world.
To those who need the thoughts
Of **love and peace and joy.**
And every thought gives rise to action,
And brings relief and pardon
For those held captive
By the thoughts of anger
And of war.

Be still a moment.
Listen to that inner **Voice** within.
For it would speak with you
And tell you who you are,
And what to do,
And where to go.
So shall you be sure of all your actions here
And know the peace,
Which surely shall be yours
When you have heard the **Voice,**
And understood the **Word**
That speaks to you.

Jan. 1999

A Note about

What Are Words?

Words are expressed by particular scribbles on a surface, such as paper, or they are sound waves created by a voice or a recording. But these "things" do not mean anything until a mind gives them meaning. But the meaning given them must go through the filters (bias or beliefs) which are part of the mind.

Furthermore, the mind does not simply give the words meaning but <u>interprets</u> what the meaning is. Thus it comes about that we often hear the comment "That's not what I meant" or "You don't understand what I'm trying to tell you".

That is why words, though one of the best means we have for communicating are not the best means of communication. Two types of communication operate simultaneously. We hear the words spoken but our minds also pick up something of the other persons thinking. So it is that we hear what is being said but we don't think it is sincere or that he means something different or he is trying to manipulate us. In other words (pun not intended) we "pick up vibes" from the other person that are not always expressed in words.

Ultimately, real communication is of the mind and is within us.

Conflict

I had a disagreement Lord.
It was a business thing
That went astray
Perhaps it was my fault;
At least, he said it was
And blamed me for it.

I suppose I am more disappointed
Than angry.
Where did I fail?
Mistakes I made;
And that is sure.
And yet the problem seems to be
More of misunderstanding.
It seems we don't communicate
The way we should.

Perhaps it is a question
Of perception.
He sees it differently than me
And blames me, for I do not see
His way.
For my part
I react,
Defend myself,
Not my fault
But rather, yours.

And so we disagree
And words go back and forth
Until eventually
We reach a compromise.

We both agree we do not like
The conflict.
But so often our perceptions
Don't agree.
Our ego's way is all we see..

We all want our own way
Because we do it best!
Others do not work
The way I do.
And I don't like it.
I want it my way.

Well, why can't I have it his way?
Would I deal with him
If his way was so bad?
Perhaps he can tell me something I can learn.
And are these situations not for learning?

Perhaps I can be at peace within myself-
Not fight against another's plans?
But weigh them carefully
Before I speak;
Passing to the One Who knows
The problem,
And from the Holy Spirit's Mind
Will come the answer that I need
To end the conflict
'twixt my brother and myself.
Here is the real solution
That we seek,
Which can bring peace to all our minds.

I know that this takes practice Lord.
For I am quick to judge
And sum up every situation for my good.

The only problem is
I do not understand the best for me.
But You do.

So will I learn to ask you first:
Will you decide for me?
And in Your Answers will I find
The answer that is best for me
And in it also will I find
The peace I need.

1998

A Note about

Conflict

It doesn't matter what situation we are in; it may be at home, at business or maybe even just by ourselves; we can be in conflict.

Conflict occurs when you get two opposite opinions pulling against each other or two different situations arise and you must decide, or someone else attacks you and you feel you must defend.

Conflict always creates lack of peace. Conflicts do not have to be "big"; small ones also destroy your peace of mind.

Conflict almost always arises because our egos want to "do it my way".

If you accept the situation without resistance and just wait and see what happens, it is surprising how things can work out. The solution will not only best for you but also for all who are involved.

Peace

If only I could be at peace awhile
And let my mind be still
And quiet.
If only I could relax and
Take away the stress.
If only I could cease the worry
And the fret of life
And just be quietly
At rest.

The daily grind goes on
The rat race pace increases till
I wonder
How best can I drop out?
How can I?
There are mouths to feed and bills to pay
And people make demands upon my time.
A never ending stream of problems
Seem to queue
For my attention.
When one is solved
Another quickly takes its place.
Where then is peace?

I find it not within
I see it not without;
For all around is violence, conflict
Bred by jealousy and anger.
If there is no peace within
Then what we see
Can only be -
War!

"Rest in peace"
they say it of the dead.

But it is not the dead
That rest in peace.
Only the living can do that.
But how?

Peace is not
The absence of war,
But
The Presence of God.
You do not need to search the world
To find the peace you seek.
It is not there.
For peace you carry with you
Deep within.

There is another way.
The quiet way of peace.
It is found in stillness of the mind.

There is another "time"
The only time there is
It is found this instant,
NOW
Within the mind.
This is eternity.

Make the time
To go within.
Only be still and listen.
This, the only rule you need observe.
And in that stillness
You will find the peace of God.
It is within your heart,
Which witnesses to God Himself. [1]

1995

---

[1]   W-p1-125.9:3
      &
      W-p1-208:4

27

A Note about

Peace

If the world is not at war we consider that we have peace. But again, real peace is nothing to do with outside circumstances or events but is within our minds. Where Peace abides there is also Love and Joy.

One of the great illustrations of peace I can recall was a picture of a severe storm and a windswept tree bent and shaking in the wind; and there in a crook of one of the branches was a nest with a bird, its head tucked under a wing and fast asleep.

Nothing external can disturb those who are truly at peace.

Peace is ultimately what we are aiming for.
Perhaps these extracts from "A Course in Miracles" shows this more clearly:

"The peace of God is everything I want. The peace of God is my one goal; the aim of all my living here, the end I see, my purpose and my function and my life, while I abide where I am not at home."

W-pl.205.1:3

"I will be still and let the earth be still along with me. And in that stillness we will find the peace of God. It is within my heart, which witnesses to God Himself."

W-pl.208.1:2

"Let me not wander from the way of peace, for I am lost on other roads than this. But let me follow Him Who leads me home and peace is certain as the Love of God."

W-pl.220.1:2

Decide For Me

Decide for me.
The way is long and tedious.
I do not see so far ahead
Nor understand the circumstances
That surround my life.
I do not have the facts,
The knowledge,
The ability,
The all encompassing wisdom,
To know
How to decide.

My fertile mind
Projects imagination
To far out limits,
To see the future
And envisage
What may lie ahead.

So often I am wrong.
I am wrong because I see
With great foreboding
Evil or disaster
Shadowing my every move;
And then I am concerned.
I worry.
Anxiety besets my heart
And grips me in its iron clasp.

Sometimes the future looks so bright and rosy
Like the sun,
Which comes up
Breaking through the clouds
To lighten up my life.

And then I feel so happy
For all seems well.
But, like the weather,
It does not last
And soon I'm back again
- To fear.

Decide for me.
I would not decide
All by myself.
I cannot.
I want to be
So independent
So able,
So competent,
So wise,
So understanding of all things.
But this lies not within my grasp.

I do not understand
What's best for me.
My decisions do not have a history
Of great success.
Decide for me.
I would do it by myself
If I but could.
Now I begin to see
This is not possible.
For I am ill equipped to make
Decisions
That will guide my life.

So many complexities
So many problems
So many things,
And people,
That project their needs
On me.

How shall I cope?
Nay, more than this,
How shall I go beyond mere coping
To a place of peace and understanding.

So You must decide.
It is not that I would not;
Simply that
I cannot.

Decide for me
In all things.
I would leave
Decisions in Your care.
For in Your Hands
The Answer lies.
You alone have knowledge
Complete and full.
You alone can say the Word
That sets me free
Enabling me to live
As You would have life be.

Decide for me.
For there is nowhere else to go
No more decisions I can make.
But place all things
Into Your care.

Indeed, I start to see
That there is not a choice
Between complexity.
There is no choice
'tween this and that,
Or one and two,
Or any opposites I know.
The choice is merely to decide
To walk the way with You.

In truth
There is no other way
That I can go.

Decide for me.
For I would go
The only way I can.
My path is sure
My way is clear,
My feet walk surely
On the road ahead.
No more the thought of future dread;
For all is in Your Hands
When you decide for me.

So now,
What more needs can be
If you, my Father,
Now,
This day,
Decide for me?

1996

Decide For Me

The basic thought behind these verses is not that we should not decide things for ourselves <u>but that we cannot</u>. That does not mean we are incapable of making decisions. Far from it. We do this all the time. The question is "Are they the right decisions? Are they the best decisions that we can make?" We do not know. We simply make the best decisions of which we are capable at the time.

The reason, of course, is that we not only do not have all the facts that surround those decisions but even if we did would we then be able to decide the best course of action for us?

There is One Who **does** know and Who **is** able to decide, and Who desires only our happiness.

Security

Security

The Love of God sustains me.
What else is there?
I have sought a thousand ways
To be secure,
To solve my problems
To impress and
Be admired.

Love was all I wanted.
It is the cry of every soul,
The universal need
That even the very young
Will die unless it is received.

I want a magic elixir
To heal my wounds;
For energy and power
To overcome all obstacles.
The world pretends to know
And advise;
To provide the facts
And all the information that I need
For happiness.

Yet such a magic potion
Does not exist.
There is no security
No freedom
No happiness
No joy
No lasting peace
In any formula this world has made.

But it exists;
The power to sustain
Against all seeming adversaries,
All adverse situations,
All the problems and complexities
That lie in wait.

It is here,
And freely given.
Not something which you buy
Or seek outside yourself.
But hidden deep within
Your mind.
In the quietness
That lies beneath the turmoil
And the strife
That bubbles in your consciousness

It is there.
Waiting for you to see it,
Be aware
And make it again your own.

The Love of God is what sustains you [1]
Nothing else is there
In which to place your faith.
You've tried so much
So often
And all have failed.

Here is the one thing
That works!
The love of God
Resolves all seeming difficulties
Without effort
And in sure confidence.

Let no foolish thoughts
Replace this one.
For here lies all you need.
In one sentence is the answer given –
The Love of God sustains me now!

1998

¹   W-p1.50.Heading

A Note about

Security

The one thing about life in this world is that we all, at some time, suffer from a sense of insecurity. A typical example is when a lot of bills suddenly come your way and you happen to be very short of funds. There comes a sense of panic, of uncertainty about the future and of your ability to cope with foreseeable events. In a word – Security.

Security means different things to different people. If you live in Afghanistan or Syria or some war torn country security may mean having a roof over your head, food to each or escape from persecution.

The world is a very insecure place.

To be confident of the future, of our relationships, our decisions, our possessions or anything else we feel we need leads to a strong desire for security.

These verses indicate the only direction that leads us to this end.

The Song

You've heard it before.
Somewhere in your memory – deep within
It lingers still
And yet
You cannot seem to quite remember exactly how it was.
The tune, the melody is but faintly remembered [1]
But now and then you hear it once again.

Perhaps it comes from music that you hear
Perhaps it comes at times when all around you Hell breaks loose
Or someone loved is ill or sad.
Perhaps it comes when you just sit and listen
Or see the rising sun
Or hear the rain upon the roof.

You maybe look at something past
The happy times of long ago
A family gathering or one you loved
Or some nostalgia triggers off a thought - and there it is again-
A wisp of melody, a song that once you sung
Uniting with those countless voices
In harmony so rich, so wonderful that cannot be described.

You feel it still.
No matter how you try to put it out of mind.
It there remains, a haunting song
That you remembered long ago
Is with you still.

What is this song?
And whence it comes?
Does it not speak of love?
Does it not bring back distant memory
Of some forgotten home?

Not this house you live in now
But that real home you knew,
That seems so long ago
But is remembered still.

It calls to you
This wisp of song;
For you can still recall the peace and joy that flowed
The harmonies that rose from million voices
Joining with one mind in glorious harmony.
There is your home,
Where there is peace
Where there is only love
And all our wills are One with His-
Our Source, Our Being and our God!
And there it is again,
The melody lingers still
Within your mind
And always will it come
Until one day you find
A great desire for where you heard that song
And sing it once again.

You do not have to leave this world to sing this song
It needs but your desire
Your willingness to be with that great throng;
And then it will be yours
And you will once again be Home
Where you belong
And you will join with all of Heaven
With One Mind, with one accord
To sing again the Song of Joy!

2009-12-29

¹   T-21.1.7:5

A Note about

The Song

Everyone has some spiritual experiences. It may be just a feeling of unexpected joy. Or maybe being by yourself in some beautiful countryside and having a feeling of being one with all of Nature around you. It may be a feeling of peace or ecstasy. There are many variations. All recognise the experience although the explanations (doctrines. theology, dogma) may vary considerably.

So it is that these verses speak of a memory of something you heard once long, long ago (or so it seems), a time when you were happy, loved and at peace. It is "our song", the memory of our real Home and our desire and search to find it once again.

Some of the other verses have the same theme, especially "Nostalgia", "The Ancient Song" and "Homeward". This theme is the driving Force behind all our searching here.

Truth 1

What is truth?
We ask the question
And then move on
Stopping not to answer.
For do we really want to know?
The truth will do no harm,
Or so they say,
But when it comes too close
We shy away,
Afraid.
We do not always want to know
The truth.

It is true
That you are reading this.
But that is not the Truth.
It is true that you
Can look into a mirror
And see reflections of your face,
But that is not the Truth.
These are but facts
And they are true as we behold them
In this world.

But Truth is something else again;
And if you want to see it
From my pen
Or hear it from my lips
You will not find the Truth.
I cannot tell you what it is
I can but point the way,
A finger, a little light, a sign
To show the way,

Pointing direction,
The way that you might go.
Do not believe the things I say,
They may be true;
But they are not
The Truth.

Truth can only be
Experienced. [1]
For Truth is what IS.
Truth and Reality are one;
For what is Real is True

And what is True is Real.
All else illusion is,
A belief firmly held perhaps
And giving rise to what seems real.
But only Truth is True. [2]

If you would know
The Truth;
Then all that which is false
Must be removed.
Truth does not change.
It stays the same
No matter what you do,
Or what you think,
Or what belief
Or understanding
You may have.
Truth still
Remains the same.
But when that which is false
Is gone
And error is no more,
Then what remains
Is Truth.

Truth has no opposite
For only Truth is True.
The opposite of Truth is false
And cannot then be real. [2]

Now only Truth remains
For only Truth is Real.
And Truth
And Peace
And Love
And God
Are all the same.

2000

[1]   T-8.VI.9:8
[2]   W-p1.152.3:6,7,8,9

A Note about

Truth 1

There are two sets of verse about Truth. When the second one was written I had forgotten that I had already written on the subject. However, it turned out that they were sufficiently different for both to be included.

The point about Truth is that no-one here can tell you what It is. I can only point in that direction, for Truth is something you must experience for yourself. It is what you are.

Time

What is time?
The passing of the day,
The seasons as they come and go?
Life, birth & death?
The cycling of the years?

Or is it like some carpet
Rolled out long, before us
As we move along its way?
Is it the space from this moment
To the next?
Or perhaps the gap between
Cause and effect?

Time is the distance
Between the past and future.
In time there is no present moment
Only the movement from here to there,
From past to future.

Time means we do not stop.
Like our minds
We are in constant motion,
Never pausing to see the vision
Of the present moment–
Now!

There is no present;
Only the past.
We guard it with
Our memories,
Our albums
Full of pictures of the way we've come.

And from these we can deduce
The way we'll go.

So we stand upon the past
And look into the future
And repeat again
The folly we have made.

Time
The guardian of our idea
Of separation.
Everything split
To years
And days,
Hours and minutes
You & me
Inside, outside
Cause and effect
Not one
But two.

Time splits us off from God.
He too is separate from us
A Being far distant
Unattainable
Unknowable
Perhaps some time
In the future
We will understand.

But, if time is past and future
How can it be at all?
The past is past.
We hold it as a notion
A memory track
A record in some book
Or on a disk.

It is not there at all
Except we think on it
And bring it into
Now
And call it real.

The future too,
Defined by us
Cannot be now;
But still awaits
A future time
For us to see.
It is not here
Except we think on it
And bring it into
Now
And call it real.

What then is time?
A notion
A figment
Of imagination
A device
Made up to serve us
In this world
There is no time.
Only eternity.

NOW
Comes close
To the Eternal Presence
Which is God
Enveloping all that IS
And you and I
And everyone.

Here is our Home
Where we belong;

In the present moment
Eternity –
The only time there is.
For this is Real
And in Reality
We really dwell
Could we but see
And understand
Eternity.

June 2010

A Note about

Time

Many have pondered as to what time really is.
We seem to know, and yet, when we come to examine it it is not so simple.

We think of time by using clocks, very accurate ones too.
But years ago there were no clocks and, in a sense, no time.
Like birds, I suppose, people got up when the sun did and went to bed soon after it set.
They knew the day was half spent when the sun was directly above them.
Later, men built sundials to show the position of the sun giving an idea of how much time was left for the day.

But time is not simply the measurement of the sun's position split into ever smaller bits.
Time is used by science to calculate, to predict, and to theorise.
But time is more than that.
We think of our past. Indeed all our thoughts are thoughts of past. Some are projected to include future events but always based on the past.
So it is that the past becomes very important to us and our memories are often used to sustain us in difficult times; hence the value placed on photographs and records of people past.

But there is also the future. We not only live in the past but also in anticipation of the future, always hoping it will be a happy time but sometimes dreading (worry, anxiety) that it may not be. And fear fills our lives because we do not live now but at some anticipated future time.

Our minds move between the past and the future.
But there is a point where there is a "crossover" - where the past changes to the future -The NOW point.

My Birthday

My Birthday

It is today my birthday.
Yet I was never born
Nor will I die.
For life is but the life of God
And lives eternally.

Who can understand eternity?
Can you make out endless time?
Day after day after day
Forever and ever;
Do you want to live this way?

Eternity is not endless time
But time that ends.
It is that small point between
The past and future.
We miss it
Always thinking of the past
And projecting to the future.
So, we say,
The past determines what we do
In future days.

But,
This is not so
For what determines what must come
Comes from decisions made today.
Today is all there is.
The past is gone
It is not there.
And, as is said,
Tomorrow never comes.

So NOW is all there is
This present moment
This is eternity
"Nothing before it, nothing after" [1]
Always now.

This present moment
My birthday.
What do I decide today?
Not something based upon the past
Not some desire for future happiness.
If happiness must be
Then
It must be today.

So, today I would be happy
How can this be?
When I am surrounded by so much misery.
For such is in this world
Where happiness is brief
Where fear is rife;
We grasp what happiness we can
And think us lucky in this life.

If I would have a happy day
Then I must find another way.
For what this world provides
By way of pleasure
Never seems to last.
The things outside of us attract
And then are past.

Lasting joy and peace
Can not be found
In things we see and hear
In touch and sound.
The pleasures of the senses
Do not bring lasting joy.

There is another way.
But it is found within
And it is here that you will find
That peace and joy
Abide
Within your mind.

So deep within my mind
Is where I'll seek,
A place of deepest peace.
And all things in the turmoil,
And the suffering,
And the conflict in this world
Are but ripples on the surface of my mind.
And nothing can disturb the peace I find
That lies eternally
Within the depths
Of Mind.

"Have a happy day"
They say.
And so I will; as I decide
To find within the joy and peace
Where happiness abides.

August 5th. 2013

A Note about

My Birthday

Birthdays keep coming!

There are overtones in these verses which are found in "Time" and also the recurring idea that all Reality is within us.

When you are young you cannot comprehend a time when you will actually leave school.

When you have finished all your basic studies the "world is your oyster", you feel maybe that you can achieve anything. Your whole life is ahead of you.

Around age 40 you start to think that maybe you are getting to the middle of your life span. You hadn't previously thought about it coming to an end.

When you get to about 70 you start to realise you body is gradually deteriorating, but "inside" you feel just the same as you ever did. Your body might be going downhill but **you** haven't changed at all.

When you get to 80 you start to recognise that your lifespan is limited and begin to tidy up your affairs and look to the future.

When you get to 90.....................

But - as E B Browning said

"The best is yet to be".

Easter
(Forgiveness)

They were talking on the radio
About forgiveness.
We should forgive as God forgave,
For is this not the message
Easter gives?

How difficult is forgiveness!
Not perhaps for small things,
But almost impossible
If one considers
A murdered child,
The torture of those you love,
The kidnap and abuse
Of those too innocent to understand;
The wholesale slaughter of millions,
The wilful starvation of cities,
The sowing of plague and pestilence,
The destruction of towns and villages,
The plight of refugees from war-
And worse;
The persecution of the Holocaust
And slaughter of the Jews;
These acts must be accounted for; but
How can they be forgiven?

And yet the teaching is that we forgive.
How can we?
We who hold resentment for
The merest slight,
Who may forgive, but not forget.
For you offend me;
And now expect me just to
Walk away,

Forget it ever happened.
You have broken links that bound us,
Your actions severed
Something deep within
That never can be whole again.

I will forgive you, for
I must;
But this cannot restore what now
Is shattered,
Irrevocably broken
By your sin.

I will forgive you –
For I perceive
You are not all bad.
There is some spark of goodness
In each one of us;
Even in you.
Because I am generous
(even, dare I say, magnanimous)
I will forgive you.

Or I may sympathise with you;
And say "there but for the grace of God
Go I."
And because I am so humble
And see my own shortcomings
In the things that you have done
I must forgive the wrong
That you have done
To me.

Is not forgiveness difficult?
It is costly, so they say,
To forgive.
It cost God the sacrifice of
His Own Son

In order to forgive
The human race.

And we, lesser beings,
Do not easily forgive.
The words come to our minds
And choke us
Even as we say
"I forgive you,
Now, today."

Why should we forgive?
If you have wronged me
Why come looking
For forgiveness?
It is only punishment you seek
Which justly is your due.
Why should I forgive?
Nay, rather, should I not assist
In punishment.
You cannot argue you deserve it not;
For you are guilty
That much is for sure!

You are thrice condemned.
You say yourself you're guilty,
And so do I.
If I forgive you, this
Becomes the third time;
We both agree your guilt
Is real,
And only I release you from it.
And seeing this,
I find that to forgive
Is difficult, indeed
Well nigh impossible!

How can some crime of great enormity
Be forgiven.
If it was my child you had destroyed
Could I forgive?
If for God
Forgiveness is a costly thing,
Then how much more
For you and I?

But yet consider this a little more-
If God forgives it means
That he was first offended:
Which is attack.
By some thought or action we,
Or other beings,
Took against Him.
By our actions we become
The enemy of God.
We have the power to attack
The One
Who created us!

How could it come about that God,
In His foreknowledge
Would create His opposite?
Something which,
Once set in motion,
Was incapable of being stopped;
And made all the evil
Of which the mind of man,
And his imagination,
Could conceive?

If God loved us,
Surely He would put a stop
To this mad rush of evil.
(For even the maddest of us

would do the same –
If we but could)
Or does He lack the power?
Or perhaps He does not care?

Yet, if God is good,
How can there be another power
Of evil,
Set against Him.
Or are there then two powers,
One for evil,
One for good –
Two gods?

Or is God not only love
But hate as well;
Like two sides of a coin?
Or perhaps, a super model of ourselves,
With good and evil intertwined within?

God then, must forgive
What He created!
For IF all power is His
Then all that IS
Is His as well.

To say He did not
Manufacture evil
But allowed it to exist,
But begs the question.
The responsibility is His alone,
Unless there is another god
Which rules the realms of demons
And disaster?

Does God then forgive
The ones that He created us to be?

Can we attack, offend, our own Creator?
Call it sin
And beg forgiveness?

What sort of God is this?
What diabolical creation has He made?
That all mankind lie heavy
With the guilt of sin
Which He allowed;
And threatens us with punishment
In Hell
(which He has made)
Unless in our contrition
And repentance
We turn again
To Him.
Is this what you call "love"?
Or should we rather fear
A god like this?

No more of this.
If this is your god
Who nails his own son to the cross
And makes demand for sacrifice until
Forgiveness is complete;
Then who is it wants the "good news"
Of their sins forgiven
To worship such a god as this?

Forgiveness can be only given
To illusions.
We cannot forgive
That which is real.
For to forgive Reality is
To forgive God, Himself.
And this
Is meaningless.

What seems so real to us
Has no bearing on Reality.
For nothing outside of you
Is real.
Only that within.
For God is Spirit.
So are you.
And Spirit only is
The One Reality.

Everything in this world
And in this universe,
Changes.
Reality alone
Changes not.

"Forgiveness is
The recognition
That what you thought
Your brother did to you
Has not occurred.
It does not pardon sins
And make them real.
It sees there was no sin.
And in that view are all your sins
Forgiven." [1]

For God IS Love.
Of this there is no doubt.
All power is His,
And He creates all things
Just like Himself.

What has all appearance
Of evil
And terror
And pain,
Has no power

And no Reality.
But do not underestimate
The power of belief in all of this.
For this alone sustains
Illusions of reality.

But One is Real,
And He does not forgive
For He does not condemn.

And when at last,
We start to see
Through tear stained, darkened eyes;
And when, at last, those eyes
Begin to wake from sleep
And start to see;
Then we perceive,
And catch a glimpse
Of our Reality.

Forgiveness then
Is really
A correction;
An undoing of error
An ability to see beyond
Appearances of evil.

Certain it is
That in this world
Bodies can be harmed,
And ego images tarnished
And affronted.
Certain it is that your belief
That you can be attacked
Will anger you,
And such attack
May harm your brother's body
Or your own.

These are beliefs
That need correction.
For there is nothing
Outside of you. [2]

Certain it is that
You can not be harmed
Or suffer loss in any way.
Certain it is that
When you understand
Your real Identity,
Who you are;
Then you will see
That you are spirit,
And Love;
Created by your Father
Like Himself.

And when at last
We all awaken from the dream
Of evil that we made;
And cease to hold belief
In guilt and fear.
Then we will see
That all God made
Was good,
And Joy
And Happiness
And there is nothing to forgive!

Aug.1998

[1]   W-p2.Intro. p1-1,2,3,4
[2]   T-18.VI.1:1

A Note about

Easter

This was written one Easter time.

Easter celebrates the death and resurrection of Jesus. It asks the question "Why was he crucified?" These verses are about that question.

Traditional doctrines about Jesus leave many questions unanswered but, in the end God **is**

All powerful

All knowing

All loving

The death of Jesus was NOT a sacrifice.

Sacrifice is loss.

God is the "Sum of All Things".

There is nothing else and therefore there is nothing that God can lose. Sacrifice is a concept totally alien to God.

His death was an extreme example to teach that the destruction of the body does not justify anger because his, and our reality, is Spirit which is indestructible. Jesus taught his perfect immunity which is also ours.

He "elected to demonstrate that the most outrageous assault, as judged by the ego, does not matter....The message of the crucifixion is perfectly clear –

Teach only love, for that is what you are.

If you interpret the crucifixion in any other way, you are using it as a weapon for assault rather than as the call for peace for which it was intended" [1]

Our reality is the same as his. We are spirit, made in the Image of God. We do not see ourselves that way because we have chosen to believe otherwise. But what God creates remains as He created it. He created us perfect, Spirit like Himself. We cannot change that, and we remain forever as he created us.

[1]   T-6.1.9:1 & T-6.1.13/14:1

Reality 1

What is reality?
You think your eyes see
And your ears hear,
Your fingers touch,
Your nose perceives
The subtle scent.

You feel the pleasure
And the pain,
And could not for a moment
Doubt your body's presence
And its reality.

But nothing in this world is stable
Or secure;
Everything changes and decays;
Everything has a cause
And seems to be separate
Within itself.

Nothing that changes can be
The Ultimate Reality.
The world that we perceive
Depends on "something else: beyond it
To sustain it.
What is this Source?

Even you, who live within this world,
Do not know who you are.
You try to find yourself
In myriads of ways,
And still you do not know.

What is your self?
The real you?
Is it the image that you made?
Which one at that?
Or is it something more?

Each of us sees differently.
Each seems to have
A different reality.
Yet these are but perceptions
Of the circumstances that surround us
And seem to be
Our own reality.

None of these is true;
None are real.
They are but each one's limited perception.
The true interpretation
Lies elsewhere.

The search for truth goes on
And science seeks to find an answer
In the world around us.
But, odd things happen
At the edge of knowledge.
Quantum effects seem strange
And somewhat unpredictable.
Smaller and smaller
All things seem to be;
But one day, in the end,
The answer will be there-
Nothing!

Seek not outside yourself.
The answer lies within.
Reality is not seen in effects;
Or physical form
For God is Spirit

And all that He creates
Is like Himself.

What He did not create
Does not exist.
Everything that He created
Exists as He created it- [1]
Spirit – like himself.

If you would find reality
The search must be within.
For here it lies;
And can be seen with Vision
Give by the Spirit.

You may continue to believe
In what you will-
In what you see around you.
You may continue to believe
You are a body and a mind,
But,
If you would find your Self
You must then look within
To see the Truth
Which is-
Reality.

1998

---

[1]   W-p1.14.1:2

A note about

Reality 1

This is the first of two chapters about Reality for it is a big subject and certainly my ramblings do not cover it! Yet the thoughts here and elsewhere express some fundamental ideas about the nature of Reality.

Science (and those of atheistic mind) believes that reality lies in physical phenomena. What you can sense or measure, what can be rationally evaluated by our minds is where reality lies. And so they seek a Theory of Everything (TOE) based on this notion. But, should such a theory ever be developed it will not even begin to touch Reality for This belongs in the physically unseen realm of Spirit.

That is what these verses are all about.

How Could I Love
One Such As You

How Could I Love One Such As You?

How could I love one such as you?
For you disgust me so.
You spend all day
Leaning at the bar
And drinking till the hotel
Closes late at night;
And then you stagger out
Intent on getting home
But end up in the gutter
Sitting in a pool of spew.
I could not love one such as you.

How could I love you?
You who are
Antithesis of all I am
And all I stand for.
You aim to cheat and steal,
Connive and think up schemes
And ways to cause your fellow man
Much loss.
All this you justify and say
You are an honourable man.
But this is not the way
I choose to go;
And these are not the things
I choose to do.
I could not love one such as you

You are the one I met the other day
Someone introduced us,
And I knew, in just that moment,
Something about you rubbed me
Up a strong, wrong way.
Maybe it was a "chemical" reaction;

Who can say
But in that moment this I knew
I could not love one such as you.

You reached the top did you?
How many people did you tread on
On your way?
Of those you left behind you say
That you are better at the job than they.
So you deserve reward for what you've done
To make your place beneath the sun.
It may be true where competition reigns supreme
That you are due whatever place you can achieve,
Yet can your ruthlessness be justified
So you can reach a place of power
Standing on the backs of those you left behind?
And do you care for those who are beneath you
Those not as strong or tough as you
Who do not care to self-destruct?
To reach "the top".
I do not care to share your view
And could not love one such as you.

From just a baby
You have made an image for yourself
Fashioned by your ego
To project to me
That which you would have me see.
And you have been upset when I've perceived
Another image,
Which you say is not the one
That I should look upon.
And you are angry if I
Upset the picture
You have taken such a long time to perfect;
And spent such care, to make it certain
All should look upon the "perfect" you.

And if I do not like the image that I view
I could not love one such as you.

Yet is this not an *image* you have made?
If that is so the image is not you,
But simply that – a mask, an image
Created to portray a picture
You would have us see.
And as I look I then begin to understand
That I have done the self-same thing as you;
And made an image of the self that I would be;
An image of the self
That I would have you see.
How could you love one such as me?

And as we strip away the masks
And look beyond what eyes can see
It may be there is "something else"
Our inner vision can perceive.
There is within each one a Self;
Real, created - not by us,
But by the Great Creator
Who fashioned each one
In His Image,
As extension of Himself.

So we must learn to look beyond
The image given by our eyes
For us to look upon;
And with our inner vision
See the real You
Dazzling in its beauty
Shining with the peace and joy
Of Love in which it was created.

This is the Real **you**
And you and I are both alike
Beloved of each other

And our Father too.
And when at last true vision comes
And clears my view
How could I *not* love
A brother such as you?

Jan.1999

A Note about

How Could I Love One Such As You

It has often been said that "all men are brothers", "love your neighbour as yourself", "see the good in people" and similar.....

How can you love other people all the time?
When you see a drunk who hasn't washed for a week, reeking of stale beer and cigarette smoke
or
maybe an old "bag lady" dishevelled, dirty and pushing a squeaking cart laden with all her worldly goods
or
maybe a very well dressed woman with much more money than you, who looks down on those who cannot afford her life style or who happen to be "coloured" or of a race other than her own.

And so the list goes on..... but – how can you love these people.

To love these is not a physical experience; it is of the spirit. They are the same as you, the same as me, but we need to look beyond the appearance to the reality of what they are. As we see their beauty so we see our own. As we love them, so we love ourselves.

Perfection

Perfection is not a simple thing;
Or so it seems.
For in this life we see much
That is removed from reaching
Anything
That we could call
Perfection.

Yet Jesus said we should be perfect
Just as our Father is perfect.
How can this be,
When all around is so
Imperfect?
If God created all perfection
From whence comes that which is
Imperfect?
And if He Himself is perfect
Why would He make that
Which seems to be its opposite? [1]

Have you seen perfection here?
Understand you that which is so clearly perfect?
Do you not the rather see
That nothing here runs true,
That everything at heart
Will all turn back
To chaos.

Men have tried for long
To make the one machine
That needs no tending
And will run forever.
Can this be done?
Is there one thing in this world

That will not change or vary,
Whose form is beauty to behold,
Whose actions never shift,
That grows not old,
Decays,
Corrodes,
Or wastes away?
It can't be done!

There is no perfection here,
Nor can there be.
How is it then that Jesus says
"Be perfect"?
Why would he ask the unattainable
Of you and me;
And cause us to reach out
To what our hands can never grasp.
And that which we can never be?

Yet, if perfection is of God
Why would He make things so unlike Himself?
If He created us in His own mould
The image of Himself,
Then how can we do other than
Conform unto the image
That He made?

And yet is seems we do.
That from perfection came
- Imperfection.
This cannot be, and so
There must be something else
We do not yet perceive.

What God did not create
Does not exist. [1]
This must be so or else there is
Another god.

And everything exists as He created it,
And so remains. [1]
Or else there is decay and imperfection,
Change and loss
In what is made.
That cannot be.

And what God makes
Is like Himself and bears the image,
And the mark of what He is.
Or else He must make that unlike Himself; [2]
Something which opposes and defies,
Antagonises
And even may destroy
Its maker.
Is this possible?

God is Spirit.
And He creates in Spirit
And in Love.
For this is what He is.
And everything that is
Is only like Himself. [2]

So He created you and me
Equal in all respects,
Extension of Himself,
- Perfect!

Whence comes then
All the imperfection,
And the sickness,
And the suffering,
And evil of this world?

Whence comes then
All the doubts,
And fears,

And pain,
And conflict
We endure?

Whence comes then
Nature, "red in tooth and claw",
The cruelty,
Hunger,
And privations,
And the loss
Which is our lot?

Is this of God?
Did He make evil,
Pain, and suffering?
Is this the love
Of which we speak?

You may hold to belief
Your will is unlike His.
You may believe you can
Do something else
Apart from him

You may believe
That you are not like Him;
That you are separate,
A law unto yourself,
A mind that is your own,
A separate self,
Able even to defy
Its Maker.

You may believe
And hold a world
Unlike the one
He made.
Belief is powerful indeed.

Your thoughts are mighty
And Illusions are as strong
In their effects as is
The Truth. ³

But what He made
IS perfect.
IS like Him.
And all belief
Of all who ever lived
Or may in future come
To live in time
Can alter nothing which is True.
But thought creates a fantasy
And where lay truth
Illusion now holds sway,
Vast and encompassing,
Impressing all that this
Is "reality"
And this the way!

But Truth is still;
Does not respond to other
Than Itself.
God has not changed
No more have you.
For you and I remain
As He created us; ⁴
Perfect and complete
Extension of Himself.

In Him we still abide
In spite of other thoughts
That we have made.
And if we seek the truth
It still is there
For each to find.

So then-
As we become aware
Of Truth;
We **know**
That He is only Love
And He created us
In Love-
And perfect
Like Himself.

1998

[1]   W-p1.167.1:6
[2]   T-10.V.5:5
[3]   W-p1.132.1:3,4
[4]   W-p1.110.6:2

A Note about

Perfection

Perfection is something we do not understand. We cannot really conceive of something perfect in this world.
For example if I asked you to describe the perfect man or woman you would probably change your mind shortly after you provided me with your first attempt.

People used to say "If you are in doubt just ask yourself – "What would Jesus do"? Frankly I could think of a number of answers and they would probably all be wrong. Yet some look upon Jesus as being a "perfect" human being. But what does that mean?

Furthermore, Jesus is recorded as saying "(You) be perfect as your Father in Heaven is perfect"-
Now how can I do that!

Yet here is the thing in a nutshell – you don't have to **be** perfect because you **are** perfect.
I am, of course, not talking about you "Jim Smith " (put in your name...) but who you really are as <u>spirit</u>. Because that is how you were created and that is how you remain. <u>That cannot change.</u>

Only Love

Only love!
Is this what makes the world go 'round
Or is it
Something else?

Only love!
Is this what your really want?
Why then do you condemn,
And make demands on others
To fulfil your will.

Only love?
Whence then comes the conflict
And the anger?
Whence the fear
That tightens like
And iron band
Across the centre of your being?

Only love?
Why then the bitter wars,
The angry words,
Resentment so long held
Against a brother;
Corroding within,
Cancer like:
The harsh recriminations,
And silent fury?

Only love?
'Tis fear that makes the world go 'round
And fear that drives
To wars
And bitter conflict.

Only love!
Yet love remains
The only present state,
Whose Source is here
Forever and forever.
Then where is fear
When love is here?
Where is darkness
When the light comes in?

Love encompasses all. [1]
Where is the space
For fear to enter in?
For there is -
Only Love.

Only Love!
What else can there be
Except some wild illusion;
The thought there could be
"Something more".

Only Love!
There can be nothing more than this.
Nothing else,
Now or ever.
For Love is God,
And God is Love,
And we are One
In Him.

1998

---

[1]   T- Introduction

A Note about

Only Love

I was listening to Nana Mouskouri singing a song called "Only Love" and as I listened I thought about Love. I knew that, ultimately, that is all there is for God IS Love and the Sum of All Things.

But as I wrote I realised that in this world Love is not the only thing. The world is not based on love but on fear, which is the opposite of love. But, as the Course in Miracles says:

.."The opposite of Love is fear, but what is all encompassing can have no opposite" [1]

It follows therefore that fear is not real. Nevertheless, from where we stand in this physical environment fear seems real and governs our lives. Fear, lack, sin and guilt lead to the conflicts, suffering and misery around us.

Yet, in spite of this, fear is *not* Real. Love is the only Reality and in all situations in which we find ourselves we need to remember that, whatever seems be the problem, attacking us, worrying us at the moment, our reality is still only Love.

[1]   T - Intro

This Is The Moment

For this moment I have lived
For this moment came I
Into this life;
To live
In this world;
To experience
This life.

Why?

There has to be some purpose
To existence
And yet within this world
It seems so meaningless
Pointless
Going nowhere;
Except perhaps
Around in circles.
History repeating itself;
Endlessly

Yet we seem to have no desire
To depart this life.
We grow old
But do not want to leave
Until our bodies can withstand no more
The onslaught and the ravages of time.

But why come here at all?
I see it clearly now.
My life's one aim has always been
To find my way back Home again.

What is this Home of which I speak?
For I have had here,
In this world, many homes;
But none of these has satisfied my longing
For my Real Home.
And this is what I seek.

This is the moment when I make the choice;
For each of us must choose
Truth or illusion-
And only one is True
And only one is Real.

The search is always
To remember Who I AM.
For enlightenment is but a recognition
Not a change at all. [1]
In this remembrance comes fulfilment
Of all my living here.
It is my choice for Heaven
Instead of Hell.

And what is Hell
But separation from God?
And what is this realm in which we live
But separate from God?
This world is not our home
We but pass through
And in the passing we must find
Our way back to our Home.
Or do we really want to do it all again?

This is the moment.
It is always <u>now</u> that you must make the choice.
For Heaven is the Home you left
And you will not be satisfied
Until at last you choose again
And find the Peace which leads you Home.

This is the moment.
There is no other time.
It can happen in an instant -
The moment that you choose to have it so. [1]

August 2010

[1] W-p1.188.1:4

A Note about

This Is The Moment

When you think about it, decisions are
always made in this moment. You can
decide to make a decision in the future
but that decision is still made now.

So if you are going to be happy, successful, or do something sometime the
"sometime" never comes. If it is important to you and you want it to happen
it must happen in this moment.

One of the purposes of time is to make decisions. If we do not decide we are
not making use of time. Everything we do is decided in this moment.

Atheist

There are those that say
There is no God
No life beyond the here and now.
And when the body dies
Then that is all.
It is the end.

And
This is a rational
And reasonable belief to hold.
For this is how it seems to be.
We live
We die
And no one comes back
To say it is not so;
Though some profess
At point of death
To see beyond the grave.

And
Some will say that Christ came back.
He came to say that
There is something else.
And some believe that this is true
But cannot prove it so.

It is irrational they say
To think that there is something else.
What grounds are there for this belief?
If God is real
What sort of God is it that causes or allows
Such lack and misery and suffering in this world
That It created.
If this is so then God must indeed

Be cruel; a merciless being,
Careless of happiness and love
To Its creation.

Yet, on the other hand
You say that God is Love.
How can this be?

Consider for a moment this:
If God be God then It must be
All powerful,
Able then to put a stop to all the evil in this world.

Or if this God
All knowing is
It must have known the outcome
That now is.

Or if, as some say,
God is but total Love
Then how can Love
Create a scene like this?

But evil and suffering exist
Therefore there is no God.

This argument the atheist declares
Is irrefutable.
You cannot have it every way.
If God is what you say
It could not have made a world like this.

And where can God be seen.
He is not here or there,
Nor up in space
Or in the deep.
You cannot see him anywhere
Within this world.

Or are we missing something?
The atheistic argument is sound
But does not cover all the facts.
A thing is not a fact just because
It can be measured.
You cannot measure thought,
Or love, or hate, or greed
Or anger
Or see inside the mind of man.
Yet these are facts
In our experience.
Emotions, thoughts and feelings
Are real and factual
To all mankind.

So there is something else.
And millions declare
In many ways,
In many forms,
That they know
There is a God.

They speak of God in different ways
And try to order and describe
Experience within.
In doing this religion has been made;
And history shows
Has not been loving, kind or peaceful.

But still with all the outward show
There still is that experience within
A mystic Presence that somehow
Speaks to those who "see"
And then they know within
That God exists.

If you look for God within this world
You will not find It there.

The world of God is deep within
Yourself
And any who would choose to look
Deep within their minds,
Stilled for a moment
Will hear "the still small Voice"
That speaks with trumpet call
And tells you It IS so.

You may believe there is no God
This does not make it true.
Belief proves neither that there is
Or not;
You may believe what'er you want
Believing does not make it so.

No,
You must go beyond belief
To knowledge.
And from within yourself
You find the knowledge
That you seek.
Here lies the proof;
All that you need
To know
God IS.

May 2014

A Note about

Atheist

Atheists commonly say that "religious" people have faith in things they can't prove.

I once came close to being an atheist myself because their arguments are so logical and are based on solid scientific data. But the data is all external, physical, as if that is the only factual information humans have.

Based on physical evidence atheists claim they can explain everything without resorting to some "god idea". An example of this is Richard Dawkins book "The God Delusion" which sets these concepts out in great detail. One cannot but agree with and appreciate the logic of Dawkin's arguments but his conclusion (and that of all atheists) rests basically on the assumption that this entire marvellous physical dimension happened without any design or thought behind it and that this <u>could</u> have happened, providing that sufficient time was allowed for it to occur.

However, given that the laws of thermodynamics indicate that all systems suffer from entropy (i.e. deterioration into chaos) unless some force/energy is applied to it, then one may ask why the universe did not remain in a chaotic state? Certainly there was (and is) plenty of energy in the universe but it had to be directed (or organised in some way) to create the form and beauty which we now observe. To say that, given billions of years (or unlimited time) chaos could transform into the present state of the universe without any design behind it takes a good deal more faith than that of one subscribing to the notion of "god". Indeed, to be an atheist requires more than that because one must also deny our inner drive towards the spiritual (which is in each of us <u>and which is what we are).</u>

Atheists assume that physical phenomena are real. And it is true that you will never find God in the material world, outside yourself.

Jesus was right when he said "The Kingdom of God is within you".

Reality is within.
That is where you will find God.
The atheist is looking in the wrong place.

To be an atheist requires enormous faith.

The Will Of God

~~feather~~

"There is no will but God's". [1]
This is what people say
And those that do believe,
Believe it to be so.

And yet they hold
As well, that
There are other wills
Opposed to His.

There is my own.
And I can countermand
God's Will
By doing what I think
Is opposite to Him.

And some say there is evil
And the devil,
Which personifies
The will of evil,
And opposite to God.

I know that when I think
I have another will
Then I have conflict.
For what is conflict
But the clash of wills.
Even in this world
I have a certain aim
And you have yours;
And we may not agree,
Then conflict reigns.

And from these differences
Do fears arise
That you will make demands of me
I cannot meet;
Or I will see some cherished idol
Slipping from my grasp.

When I want my will
I find that there are those
Opposed in thought to what I want.
From this comes fear,
And stress,
And anger.
From this comes attack
And grievances
And pain.
From this comes
Resentment
Worry
And the fear of loss,
And all the negatives of life
That cause us sickness, pain
And death.

And yet will I persist
In wanting what I want,
Because I think that there
Lies happiness
If only I can get it right
The next time.

There is always a "next time",
And another, and another;
But nowhere do I find the peace
And happiness I seek.
For it lies not within <u>my</u> will.

There is no Will but God's. [1]
Whilst we believe that we can see
Another will
We but delude ourselves.
And our belief that there is something else
That can oppose the will of God
Creates in us perception of reality
That is not there!

Poor fool!
How can I, mere mortal man
Oppose the Will of God.
And how can any other being
Or idea
Be opposite to His;
Creator of ALL
And Sum of ALL things
That exist. [2]

How can some little ripple
On the bosom of the ocean
Believe that it is on its own,
Independent of that great mass of water
Controlling all it does
And is?
No more can you or I
Oppose the Will of God.
It is a notion far too fanciful
Too farfetched,
Full of delusion
And madness,
Fit only for insanity.
Yet this we do believe
And hold
That we can do something other
Than what He Wills.

From this comes great illusion
And perception of our own reality,
Our little world of weakness
And of loss.
Not Real, but seeming to be so,
Perceived by us as what we want,
And can create
All on our own.

This leads us not to peace
But misery.
For what is outside His Will
Does not exist
And cannot bring us peace.

There is no will but God's, [1]
And in His Will we find
All conflict gone.
There is no Will but God's.
Here conflict thoughts are meaningless
And nothing can disturb the one
Who understands
There is no Will but His.

God wills peace for all His children;
Such as you.
And you will come to see
Your will
The same as His.
For only here lies lack of conflict,
Peace
Happiness
And Joy.
All these are given you,
Are yours,
Because it is your Father's Will
That it be so.

There is no Will but God's.[1]
Peace has replaced
The strange idea
That you are torn
By goals conflicting with each other.
For this idea is wholly true,
And no illusions can arise
When we hold nothing but
His Will.

Without illusions
Conflict is no more.
For in His will
Is only peace.[2]

1998

[1]   W –p1.74.3:12
[2]   T-29.II.10:3

A Note about

The Will of God

Some say God is **all** powerful but that there is a <u>power of evil</u> and even <u>my own power</u> can oppose the will of God.

Therefore God becomes only the **most** powerful. **If** there are powers other than God's then He is not **all** powerful.

This is not a play on words; it cannot be otherwise.

We are free to believe what we like (whether true or not) and to think what we like, and all our thinking creates form at some level. We create the conflict and misery because we think there is some other will. But truly -

There is no Will but God's.

And in this there is peace.

The Ancient Song

The Ancient Song

Last night I went to see them
And listen to their songs
They sang the old refrains
Of long ago
That triggered in my memory
Scenes from the past
For something left behind and lost.

What is this music
Which brings a lump into the throat
And tears behind the eyes.
Is it identity,
A joining
Of you and me?

There is so little in this world
That brings us all together
Yet when we hear the music
That we all know,
We join together
And let the music
Carry us along
On wings of song;
Emotion
Soaring
Gliding
Flying
In love and joy
Expressed in song.

What is this music
But an expression
Of the soul?
And it is here

That we are one
For only minds can join [1]
And when we see our oneness
Barely recognised,
Something more intuitive;
We want to be there
We want to join with others.
We recognise the song;
Not the one being played
But something more ancient,
So well known
Yet not able to be grasped
But it is there! [2]

So we join together
Thinking it the song
We're hearing with our ears.
But what joins us is the knowledge
Of the deeper song
Which we all sang together long ago,
Rejoicing then in what we were,
No - what we *are*,
And we remember still fragments
Of that song.
It comes to us unbidden
When seeing a sunset,
Or our loved ones face
Watching our children play
Or walking through a forest
Or looking at the sea
Or listening to a song.

It comes to us and we remember
That there is something
We have lost.
We know that we were happy
When we sung that song [3]
And then we lose it

And sink back to what we see;
Yet this we know does not
Bring happiness
But only misery.

So would we leave this world
And find the love and joy
Which all men seek,
Yet few there are that find.
But it is there!
If you but seek the truth
It will be found
For it is not far from each of us
If we but turn
And look within.
For there
In quiet
If we listen
We will hear it once again
The wondrous song of Love
Which we all sang together
Long ago.

1   T-18.VI.3:1
2   T-21.1.7:5
3   T-21.1.6:3

A Note about

The Ancient Song

There are some similarities in these verses to, for example, "The Song" but yet they express some further viewpoints.

The concept here is similar to that expressed in a small booklet which is an extension of "A Course in Miracles", called "The Song of Prayer."
In the introduction is says:

"Prayer is the greatest gift with which God blessed his Son at his creation. It was then what it is to become; the single voice Creator and creation share; the song the Son sings to the Father, Who returns the thanks it offers Him unto the Son. Endless the harmony and endless, too, the joyous concord of the Love They give forever to Each Other. And in this creation is extended."

Deep within our minds we hear again some snatches of this song; we remember it with love and turn again – Homeward.

Loneliness

I sat today
And for the first time
For as long as I can remember
I felt lonely.

I have often been alone.
But being alone is not
To be lonely.
To be lonely means to feel bereft
Of company
Of those your love
Of someone to talk to
Of someone who needs you
And wants you.

Being lonely gives a feeling of being alone.
One can be alone and yet not feel alone.
Feeling alone makes one
Depressed
Because of the uselessness of it all.
Nothing to do
Nowhere to go
No one to care for
No one who cares.

Even work does not stop
The ache within,
Though dulls it for a while.

Yet, why am I so?
Because my family has moved away
And I feel the pain of loss.
Or perhaps for you a loved one gone

Whose loss you feel?
And you are lonely.

Yet, why am I so?
Do I need bodies around me
To be comforted?
Do I think a moment that
A body will give me what I want?
This seems to be the case
But then I know that even in a crowd
Of bodies all around me
I am still alone.

It is the mind that thinks alike,
Along with me;
Not just the mind of man
But that extension of the spirit
Which joins one with the other.
This is what I need.
Not simply to be in touch
With bodies.
But to be in touch
With minds
That love
And care
And communicate with me.

Whence comes this communion?
It is not of the intellect
But of the spirit.
It is not the communication
Of the idle chatter
Over cups of tea,
Or gossip
With a neighbour
Or passing time of day
With someone in the street.

It is something more than this you want.
We do not want to be alone
You and I.
And we are not.

You cannot be alone.
It is not possible.
For the Spirit and the Mind
Of God, your Father,
Always speaks to you
And comforts you,
And leads you on.
His is the Gift above all gifts
Which can bring only
Joy and peace.

But, this seems to us so distant
Not real
Not achievable.
We want something,
Someone we can feel and touch.
We look for bodies for our comfort
For we think in them
We find our needs are met.
Yet this can never be,
For true communion
And love,
Are never of the body.
Seek your solace then
Where it can be found.

The Mind of Spirit
Is the only place
Where our minds
Find their rest.
For we are unaware that all around us
Are our brothers;

Who would commune with us
If we but listen.

For Mind is One.
We are a part of that One Mind
Which is extension of the Father's.
Even those we see as bodies
Those nearest and dearest to us
Are but effects and symbols
Of something greater
And far beyond
Our eyes ability to see..
Form is not reality,
But spirit is.
And thus it is to spirit we must go
If we would feel the pangs of loneliness
No more.

This is not easy.
We are accustomed to see things through
Our body's eyes,
And value form as being
The Reality we seek.
But, be assured, it is not there.
'Tis only spirit that can satisfy
The longing
And desires
And yearnings
Of the heart.

For you were made as part of Him.
Your mind extension of His Mind
Your being part of His.
And you are spirit
Along with each of us
And all your brothers.
And in this place
No one can be alone

Or sorrowful.
For here we communicate
One with the other.
Here is communion
Here is love
Here is joy
And peace at last.

- 1997

A Note about

Loneliness

I can remember being sent off to boarding school. I was seven. I was homesick.

There is not much difference between being homesick and being lonely; or maybe between loneliness and nostalgia. And, as you know, you can be lonely in a crowd of people.

Being lonely always contains the wish that you want to be with someone else, somewhere else and you can remember when you were happy then.

But the truth is we need never be lonely when we begin to understand that our reality is spirit and our communion is ultimately with the Mind of God which we all share.

Truth 2

It is too hard to understand
The way you speak.
You say that what I see
And feel;
The experiences of this life,
Its ups and downs,
Its tragedy and suffering,
And all the pain,
And all the pleasure,
And everything that happens in this world
Is nothing?

I cannot understand.
How can one deny
The pain or pleasure
That he feels,
And say it is not real?

And it is true,
That whilst we see ourselves
As body and as mind
Then to deny the feelings of the body
Is nigh impossible.

But then to each of us
At some point in our lives
There comes a sense
We do not know or understand
Ourselves.

And so we set about
"To find ourselves";
As if we, the living,
Do not live
And do not know

Exactly what we are
Or why we're here
Or where we're going.
Yet every other creature
Seems to know its place
And goes about its business
Content in what it does-
Except ourselves.

We seem to come
From places all unknown
And where our journey ends
We cannot comprehend.
Yet we perceive
That there is "something else";
A something, like a memory,
Of times long past,
And ancient story,
A wisp of melody
Returning to our minds.

And we begin to see at last
That deep within us lies
The Source of Life
And what we are.

Reality lies not outside ourselves
But deep within.
It is not form
But spirit.
And here is Truth.
Truth is not the "fact"
Beloved of the intellect
Truth is not written down
For all to read,
Recorded in the annals of mankind.
But Truth is what is Real
And lasting,
Experienced,

Made known within the mind
By Spirit
By Oneness
With the Source of All.
It is not something far away
But is within.
For you, yourself,
Extension of Reality,
Are part of Him
Who is the Sum of All.

You are the Truth
And you the Way.
It lies within;
And it is what you are
For Love created all things
Like Itself.

But this you will not see
If you would see the world
And look for lasting joy
Outside yourself.
For it is true
That there is nothing there!

All things you see
And feel and smell and touch
Will pass away.
None of this will last-
And cannot.
It is not simply made of dust;
It is not made at all.
And all of form remains
One vast illusion;
Magnificent in its ability
To witness to reality
Of something great and wondrous
That does not exist.

What God created
Only has Reality.
And He created you
And you remain
As He created you. [1]
You have not changed
And sinned
And separated yourself
From Him or from each other.
You have not grown weak
And lacking anything you need.
For all is yours
Given you at your creation,
And so it still remains.

You will not see all this,
Will fail to understand
The simple Truth.
For Truth cannot be sought or found
Or written down,
But it must be
Experienced. [2]

If you would find the Truth
Then willingness must be your guide.
For many say they want to know
But their desire is still
For "something else",
Believing that
There is some other thing
Some other circumstance
Event
Or person
Or possession
That will make them whole
And thus complete.

It is not so.
You must be willing
And desire to know
The Truth
That sets you free.

For Truth
And Joy
And Peace
And Love
And Freedom
Are all the same
And freely given
All who seek
In earnestness
To find the answer
That is already theirs.

Truth is true.
It has no opposite.
For what is opposite to Truth
Is false,
And so, unreal.
This is the simplest
Of all distinctions
We can make-
And yet we do not understand. [3]

Truth is true.
And nothing else exists.
For Love encompasses all things
And there is nothing else
Nor e'er will be.
And yet within Itself
It has no limit.
And you exist
Within this One Reality

Without limit
Everywhere and everything
Creating like Itself
Eternally.

2001

[1]   W-p1.94.3:3
[2]   T-8.9:8,9
[3]   W-p1.152.3:5 & 4:1

A Note about

Truth 2

This is the second set of verses about Truth.

- Truth and reality are the same.
- What is True is Real and what is Real is True. We are here talking about Ultimate Reality. What our body's senses tell us seem to be real. But this is perception. And perception can change.
- Reality can not change. It is the Basis, the Source, and the Sum of All Things.
- Truth cannot have an opposite.
- The opposite to Truth is untrue (unreal, non-existent)

To determine our perception our senses feed us information and our minds interpret what we see, feel, hear, taste and smell and from that determine what is there. That is why not everyone sees or feels the same about anything. Our internal "filters" are all different and therefore our interpretations all vary, sometimes only slightly.

Furthermore, our perceptions (our "reality") changes with time or changing circumstances. What we saw, believed and acted upon when we were 20 is likely to be quite different when we are 50 or 80....

So these verses are about Truth.
It is true that leaves are green and the sky is blue (well it mostly is where I live!) but that is not the Truth. Truth is beyond the sun and stars and the physical universe. All this comes from spirit and it is there we experience Truth.

Truth is not the prerogative of any person. It is available to all who would look within. It requires only the sincere desire and the willingness to do so.

Worry

Anxiety is a form of fear
It comes to all of us.
We are fearful
For our family
Our friends,
Ourselves.
We know not what the future brings.
But it brings -
Disaster!

Always there is something coming.
Because it is unknown
The dread is worse.
That which is good and happy
Cannot continue.
The disaster must visit us
Sooner or later.
And we fear its coming.

Yet somehow, when it comes,
We handle it.
We have always managed,
Coped,
Handled the situation.
We're still here aren't we?
But we may have been happier
Had we not worried.

Why are we so fearful?
Did God create fear?
How could he?
He Who is Love cannot create its opposite.
Would God create something
So unlike Himself?

Something so totally opposite
It could even destroy its Creator?
How foolish are our thoughts!
That which God did not create
Does not exist. [1]
Where then is fear?

You may continue to believe
In what is not real,
Nor has existence of itself.
Fear is not real
Except you give it power.

Nor has it power over you
Unless you permit it so.
You do not have to believe
In what is not true.
Unless you choose it so.
This is the Spirit's Law:
The choice is always yours.

Shall we continue then in fear,
To worry and be anxious,
The guilt of past events
Which now are past and gone forever;
Or live in trepidation
Of what is yet to come?
If it does, it may not be
The form you thought.
It could end up as something quite benign;
It could be worse!

But there is nothing in this world
You cannot handle.
The strength will always be there,
The power of God Himself
Lies in you.
Look within,

For there the Presence is
Of One Who loves you.

Be not fearful then;
For there is nothing to fear.
You have His Word,
His promise
This is so.

And everywhere you go
Whatever you do
Wherever you are
There also is your Friend
Who walks with you.

1998

¹   W-p1.14.1:2

A Note about

Worry

We were waiting at the airport. The plane was late. There had been some mechanical problem which delayed the flight.

But then they were there and we all went home to be greeted at the door by a waiting mother.
"Where have you been?"
We explained – and then she said, "I wish you had phoned and told me. I could have worried about it!"

We all have some idea that our worrying somehow helps the situation. Worry is a form of fear. It does nothing constructive and, indeed, may cause us to make the wrong decision.

Unfortunately we all tend to worry, but we don't need to. That is what these verses are all about.

When Fear Has Gone

There is no fear just now
For fear is only of the past
And future,
Which do not exist.

There is no fear.
If this be true
How is it then the whole world
Runs on fear.
Not simply stark terror
Or the knot within the stomach
Or the splitting head
Calling for relief from fear.

Fear shows itself
In anxiety
Worry
Anger and impatience,
Resentment,
Sacrifice and loss;
In jealousy
And malice
And a mere slight twinge
Of annoyance. [1]

There are a thousand ways
That fear is manifest;
For all that is not love
Is only fear
And can be nothing else

So fear abounds around us
In this world.
In all the negatives of life,

The weakness
And the dreariness,
The threats of others
And their steady unforgiveness
Pinning you to guilt.

But if there is no fear
How is it that we feel it so?
Why does it persist within us
Creating great unhappiness?
How can we rid ourselves of this
And live our lives in peace and happiness
Without the blight of fear
In all its forms?

Fear lives within the bounds
Of past and future.
This is time
Where man exists
To live in misery a while
And then to die.
But what is time?
If the past is over
And the future yet to be
Then all that then remains
Is "Now".
And time has gone.
With its departure then goes fear
For in the present
Fear does not exist.

We live in time.
We see continuity
Of past and present,
And project into the future.
Fear lives within us
And dominates our lives.
But this need not be so!

Reality does not lie within the past
Nor in the future.
Reality is what IS,
And what IS
Is Now.
All else outside the present
Is perception,
Interpretation,
And time and fear
Are all a part
Of this illusion.

Tis here we seem to live
In weakness
And in fear;
Impaired of vision
And the power of Spirit.
Guilt reigns supreme
And powers the fear that
Drives the sorrows of this world.

The Love that casts out fear
Is not within this world.
There is another world from whence
Comes power to banish fear forever,
And within our lives today.

This Love is God
And God is Love,
And this is what you are;
Extension of Himself.
We do but sleep
And do not see or understand
The offer of His Gift.
For all He gives is Love.
To be aware of this

And feel it in ourselves
<u>Must</u> banish fear.
And what remains is only
Love.

[1]   W–p1.21.2:5

A Note About

When Fear Has Gone

Everyone feels fear at some stage. This is generally attributed to what we would call a fearful situation. But fear is more than this. It underlies the whole world. All the systems and beliefs of the world have an underlying fear and from this come wars, anger, resentment and all the negatives of life- including death- and with all these an underlying guilt. We do not want this situation.

Fear and love cannot co-exist. We all need love. For where love is there is no fear. In the world you seem to see many forms of love. There is the love of a mother for her child, the love of a man for a woman, the comradeship that binds two men in friendship, the love that sacrifices for another, the love that is always there to help you when you need it. These "forms" of love can be of great benefit to us but do not destroy the underlying fear.

All these forms of love are not what destroy fear. What we need is the "perfect Love that casts out fear". This is found only in spirit. It is what God IS and in Its Presence all darkness disappears.

Reality 2

"Nothing real can be threatened
Nothing unreal exists
  Herein lies the peace of God." [1]

What is reality?

What is real to you
May not seem real to me.
We each create our own
Reality –
So they say.

Yet, is this true?
If reality is different for me
-Or you
Does this not mean reality can change?
And any view I have seems real to me.
Or does this simply mean that nothing
Is really Real
And everything can change?

If reality can change then
Is it really Real?
Is it possible that the Ultimate Ground of All things
Can change?
For surely what is Real must be the
Rock for all that IS?
The search goes on.
For all agree there must be something there;
Something that is the ultimate base of all there is.
At first it was the atom
That particle, which no one could divide

The base for matter,
You and me,
Everything

They found the atom.
And then within
A proton and electron
And a host of other particles beneath.
Where will it end?
Somewhere there must be
That which is the ultimate
Reality

When that is found
It will not change
For it is then the Source of All that Is
And all existence stands upon
Reality

If this is so then
What is Real can not be
Threatened or destroyed,
For if it were then all
Would disappear.

That which IS
Is Real
And stands forever.

But what of all our world
That changes by the instant?
What is today is not the same
As yesterday.
And tomorrow will be different still.
We each see something different
That changes as our senses feel
The world outside.
What minds interpret is but

Perception
Not Reality.

So, if it changes
And is not real,
Then what is that we see?
Does it exist?
Of course it does –
Or so it seems to us.
But we – our bodies
Also change
And all goes back
To dust.

If all things change and
All else decays;
Can this be real
Or just illusion
Of Reality?

It seems so real!
The test of good illusion
Is appearance of reality.
It seems so real!
But is this so
Or just perception
Of our desires and senses?

Are we illusions too?
Do we exist?
Are we but bodies
That decay and die
Or something more than this?

We know we live.
Our bodies change with time
But somehow we do not.
Within me is an "I" that still remains

The same;
And changes not.

I know that this is Real;
And will remain when time
And change have gone -
I will remain.

The Me that IS
Is Real and nothing
Can attack or threaten
Me.
I exist.
I am
And changeless I remain
Through all Eternity.

October 2013

A Note About

Reality Two

This, of course, is the second set of verses about Reality. It goes to the basis of what might be called Ultimate Reality.

In this world we each seem to have our own sense of reality and each one is different. Furthermore, our idea of reality can change. This is not reality but perception. But to us it seems so real.

Ultimate reality is what IS. It cannot change.

All else is illusion.

Feelings

Feelings

Sometimes things happen
Which cause a sudden feeling
Of depression
Or joy
Anticipation
Or relief;
A moment of regret,
Uplifting of the spirit,
Back & forth
Up & down
Never stable.

Emotions
Come and go,
Reactions to what happens,
Circumstances
Out of our control;
Things
Causeless,
Or at least
Not of our doing.
So are we swept along
Seeming victims of events
Beyond control.

Must we then continue
As victims?
Only responding
When disaster strikes,
Or good news comes
Into our lives.

'Tis just chance
That guides us,

And sometimes
We are lucky,
And sometimes not.

There is no chance.
Nothing happens
Without cause
And nothing's caused
Without intent.
Intent comes from the mind.
Nothing happens
Without ideas.
Ideas are of the mind
And come from nowhere else.

You are not helpless
In the scheme of things.
For mind controls
All that we see
As reality.

Deceive yourself no more.
You have the power
Within your mind
To change your life.
You are responsible for what you see
You choose the feelings that you feel
And every goal that would be yours,
And all that happens to you,
Is your decision.
You ask and you receive
As you have asked. [1]

The thought comes first,
Well in advance;
Held firmly in the mind,
Held with desire
It gains in power,

And then brings forth
The action
Or event
Which we desired.

Emotions come & go
One high for many lows.
But this is not the way
You want to go.

Joy can be constant.
Peace within;
Stability;
Surrounded by
The Love of God.
The choice is yours.
The power of your mind
Is one with His.

Jan.1999

A Note about

Feelings

I always wanted to know "the answers". I searched all the books and information I could, and eventually came to the conclusion that I knew all that I needed to know.

But that wasn't enough. There was something missing. To know intellectually did not give me the real Answer. I had to go beyond that to the Experience – to the experience of what I knew to be true.
The knowledge was not in the intellect it was in the experience and the experience is through feelings.

Emotions are of the body.
Feelings are of the spirit.

If, in this life, all we come to is a feeling of peace that cannot be disturbed in any way then joy and love come with that.

Nothing more is needed.

Belief

You say "Believe"
And you will see the truth of what is said.
But why "believe"?
Is not to know the facts enough?
I have searched.
I know the reasons why
I know the details of the path
That I have chosen.
Why then this need
To believe.

If I have the intellect
To understand the "mysteries"
To see the reasons why
Things are as they are;
What will belief add to my knowledge?

Knowledge without action
Is impotent.
It achieves nothing.
The question then becomes
"What must I do to experience
That which I already "know"?"

Belief is what takes knowledge
To experience.
Experience is awareness
Realisation of the truth
Of what you think you know.

Oh yes, I know that you believe
All that your mind holds to be true.
But you will never know the Truth

Unless experience leads you
To awareness.

Belief leads to experience.
Experience is the key
To understanding.
Understanding leads to
Knowledge of the Truth.

How then do I believe?
Do I simply put my trust
In what I'm told?
I do not want to blindly
Believe some doctrine,
Dogma, theory, or accept
What someone else believes
Is true.
They may be wrong.
How then can I believe
And put my faith
In what is Real and True?

There comes a time
When all your searching
Reaches to a point
Where you can go no further;
Where everywhere you look
You see the same ideas
Perhaps in different form.
But you know the way
Your path has led
And brought you to this point.

And, deep within,
There comes a certainty
About the things
You think you know.
Experience is what is needed now.

To perceive the truth
Is not the same to
Know it. [1]
Truth cannot be perceived,
But only known. [2]
Nothing is so easy
To recognise,
As truth.
This is the recognition
That is immediate, clear and natural [3]

So now there is a step
That I must take
That I may truly
Realise all that I know.
This step is called
Belief.

But how?
Truth does not need belief
To be Itself.
It simply IS. [4]

Truth is then merely
The acceptance
Of what IS.

This is the most natural
Easiest thing to do;
And yet we find it difficult.
But why?
We have our eyes on other things.
That which we value in this world
Becomes the block to Vision
And to knowledge of the Truth.

Our willingness to change
Is needed now.

Let go now, with confidence,
The things outside your mind
And turn within
Here lies the Experience
Which is
The Truth. [5]

For just an instant,
Now
Accept that this is True
And Real.
This is the belief
The step you need to take.

It is only the desires
Of the body
That keeps you back.
And yet you see within
The light and peace
You want above all else.

Why stop now
And teeter on the edge.
The Love, the Joy,
The Peace of God
Awaits your leap.
Have faith.
Believe it now,
For just a moment
- And you will Know.

May 2014

[1]   T-3.III.5:13
[2]   T-26.VII.3:6
[3]   T-7.XI.5:8
[4]   T-29.VIII.5:7
[5]   T-8.VI.9:8

A Note about

Belief

From a spiritual viewpoint learning is not Knowledge.

You can learn all there is to know. You can explain the most difficult questions. You have great knowledge from your learning, but even in this world we are aware that it is not sufficient to know; it is essential that that knowledge is translated into action. We learn that we might achieve.

In this world we have to search. Many have no idea what they are really searching for. Those that do know are like you who are reading this. You want to find "the answer", the ending of your search.

The answer is not in knowledge as we understand it. The Knowledge of the spirit is in experience, in feelings and awareness (not emotions). It is the experience, the expression, of love, joy & peace. This experience comes from letting go of all your old beliefs and for one "leap of faith" - that you remain as God created you – perfect, holy, limitless and unchanging – like God Itself, Whose Extension you are.

Choice

Choice

I would choose today
The way that You would have me go.
My mind has so much thought
All mixed up, confused,
With what I have to do.

I cannot just sit still today,
For when I do I'm pressed
By all the things demanding
My attention.
So much to do.
Where should I start?
What should I do?
What is the way
That I should take today?

I know that if I choose
The way I take
There are so many more
Mistakes I'll make.
Then let me just be still awhile
And let me make a space
Within my mind.
To clear the thoughts
That would intrude
Disturbing peace
Creating chaos,
Making havoc
Of the day ahead.

It seems that many roads
Branch out in front of me.
Which one should I take?
How should it be?

So much holds attraction
Seems to promise
Satisfaction
Or some trivial happiness
If I so choose.

And yet I know
That this is just not so.
All roads lead
Nowhere
-but one.
And this the one that I must take;
For here in truth
Lies happiness
And joy.
On this road
Is the satisfaction
And completion
That I seek.

And so I choose today
To go the way
That you would lead.
I choose to let You make
Decisions
In my stead.
I choose to place the future
In Your Hands
And let go all
My other plans.

For these will fail
And only Yours remain.
For mine have nowhere else to go
But to illusions
And the dreams of wealth and happiness.

But I would choose to follow You.
For Your decisions
Lead me on the road
Where all is peace
Which cannot pass away.
And what I build with You
Remains and grows
And joins with others
Until we come to that one Mind
Which is Your Own.

And so I choose to follow You
And make the only choice I can.
What else is there apart from this
And where else can I go?
And I would walk with You this day
And follow gladly
In the way
That You will choose
For me.

A Note about

Choice

Stress is often cause by having a multitude of things to do, all supposedly "urgent" and demanding immediate attention.

We think we are logical, rational creatures capable of making the "right" decision. But when you are confronted by multiple choices, which is the one you should choose?

So it is that as you look back over your life, how many choices do you think were the "right" ones? How many times have you said "If I had my life to live over I would do things differently".

Every moment of the day we are faced with choices. It is only as we choose the inner Voice to guide us that we can really make the right choice in whatever situation we find ourselves. This "Voice" comes to us in many ways. Sometimes It is heard by way of intuition. If ever you have conflict between what your reason and logical thinking tells you to do and what you inner intuition says. Be assured your intuitive response will always be the way to go.

Now

You look for guidance in the days ahead;
For there are many things you must decide.

All my thoughts of misery and despair,
Of unhappiness and despondency
Of inability
Or inaction
Or motivation
Stem from
Thoughts of past events
Of what has brought me to this point.

The past weighs on my mind
It holds me down,
It stifles energy,
Creativity,
It makes me want
To sit
And do nothing.

Thoughts of the past
But make me think I am
The ego image of myself.
And I begin to think
The sum of all these thoughts
Is what I am.

Or yet again,
I sit here
Anxious
About what may come
From some event
Projected from my past
And on into the future.

Maybe it is about
Security,
Finance,
Emotion,
My job
Or some possession,
A situation
A legal battle
Or censure of one's peers-
A thousand small scenarios
Projected from my mind.

And as I think these thoughts
I am not happy.
How can thoughts of losses past,
Achievements
Or success
Bring happiness today?
I recognise
Whatever way I see myself
As having been;
It still is past.
What have I got just <u>now?</u>

I look at all the scenes around me now;
How will they all turn out?
My present situation seems to be
The sum of all my past events,
Which bring me to this point of time.
And from this point I can imagine it,
Conjecture,
Visualise in any form
Or vision
That I choose;
And almost all are fearful.

What else is there except to find
Delight in what is <u>now.</u>

Rare is the event that comes about
The way we think.
Sometimes they are better
But most often – worse!

But peace of mind
Does not depend
On things external.
The mind within determines
Whether we see
All our circumstance
As pleasant,
Unpleasant,
Good or bad,
Happy or sad;
And we can choose.

If then,
You are not happy now
Then choose again,
Let go the past
Which brought you here,
Let go all thought
Of future gain
Or loss,
And dwell a while in the delight
Of "Now".

For "Now" is not a part of time
But of eternity.
It is not affected by the past
Or future;
And once you let these go
All that remains is this one golden thread
"The little breath of eternity
That runs through time
Like golden light
Is all the same,

Nothing before it
Nothing afterwards". [1]

"Fear is not of the present
But only of the past
And future,
Which does not exist.
In the present
Fear does not exist". [2]
And the present extends
Forever,
Nothing
But happiness
Is there.
No darkness is remembered
And Immortality
And Joy
Are **now**!

Jan. 1999

[1]   T-20.V5:8
[2]   T-15.1.8:2

A Note about

Now

A very well known book by Eckhart Tolle called "The Power of Now", and subsequent writings brought the concept of "Now" - the present moment, to people's attention.

These verses might be seen as a sort of commentary on Now.

Essentially Now is the only "time" there is. It is always there because it is infinite.

If you think about it neither past nor future exist, except as memories or projections in our mind. But always there is this present moment
- Now

Christmas –
The Christ has come

Christmas – The Christ has come

The Christ has come.
What difference does it make?
We tell the story of the little baby
Born in Bethlehem.
As if this makes some difference to the world.
For just a little while,
Once a year,
We say "Goodwill to all"
And "Peace on earth"
As if this all meant something.

And yet it does.
For even in the midst of wars
Have men stopped briefly
In their fighting
To bid each other "Merry Christmas"
And then next day
Gone back to killing.

The Christ has come.
"So what?" they ask,
The story says
He even died a bloody death
Of pain and suffering.
And from that time 2000 years ago
Has there been peace on earth?
Hardly.
Even his followers have killed each other;
Persecution, intolerance, bigotry
And splits within
Have caused great conflict
In the name of One Who only came
For peace.

The Christ has come.
Does God control this world?
They say He made it so He must.
What sort of god is in control
Of pain and famine,
Bloodshed, suffering and lust.
The Christ has come-
Does He control it thus?

The Christ has come.
But have men changed?
Where is the peace
That Christmas talks about.
The names ring out –
From Flanders fields to Vietnam,
Korea, Bosnia and Iran
And Britain and Berlin.
Of Dachau, Auschwitz,
KGB and Secret Police
Of dark and hidden places in Cuba and the Argentine.
The Christ has come.
Is this what peace is all about?

The Christ has come.
But still the world
Moves slowly on its weary way.
It is tired now
And all within decay
With rotting thoughts and twisted limbs
And fearful thoughts that lead the way
And grip the heart.

The Christ has come.
What difference does it make?
If I cannot be happy in this world
A thousand Christs may come and go
And still change nothing.

Why should I care
Or notice what such people say?
They tell me there is peace on earth
That does not come my way.
The Christ has come.
Why should I care?

The Christ has come.
What did you expect?
A trumpet sounding
And in clouds descending
To sit upon a mortal throne.
Then look in vain
For you will not see Christ with mortal eyes
Nor gain your happiness
Through some supposed happy home
Upon this earth.

You will not find it here
For Christ does not come to an earthly realm.
How can He?
This world sets out to separate itself
From all that speaks of love and joy.
It wraps itself in fear
And prides itself on being different
To all that speaks of love and joy.
How could Christ find a home
In such a place as this
Where men will boast another will but His
And then set out to find the peace of God?

The Christ has come.
Seek not to see him sit upon
Some earthly throne
And make a heaven of this world.
Such things can never be
The Source of all reality.

The Christ has come
And still remains
And so we ask each Christmas day,
With hope within our hearts –
"Will anything be different now?"

The Christ has come.
What difference has it made?
You do not see
Because you do not look
Where He abides.
I too have looked within
And seen distress;
And looked within
And there saw nothing less.

The Christ has come.
His coming made a difference
        - To me.
A small event perhaps
In the great scheme of things;
And yet it changed my life
And set my feet upon another path
That leads to love and joy and happiness.

The Christ has come.
You see
It made a difference to me.
The Christ has come
And changed my life.
There is no fear in death
And fear itself has lost its sting.
And I am not alone.
The Christ has come.
He lives in me
And I in Him
And I have found my home.

The Christ has come.
If it was only me
Then where is hope
For all the millions of this world
Who walk alone
In sorrow and in suffering?

But He has come.
And all of those who tread the path
And follow
Like Wise Men
The road that leads them
To the stable
And the manger
And the baby,
Will find the difference
That His coming makes.

The Christ has come.
You will not find Him
In the markets and the money
Of this world,
Nor in the glitz and tinsel
Or so called "pleasures"
That it offers you
On every hand

You will not find him
In the places
Or the palaces
In the power
Or the status
Or possessions
Or the pleasures
Of the senses
That pervade the world
In which we stand.
He is not there.

And yet
The Christ has come.
And will be found
By all who seek for Him.
The Christ has come.
And you will find Him
When you look for Him
Within your heart.

The Christ has come.
And still remains.
He travels with you all unseen
Until you want to waken from your sleep.
And when at last
You turn your dreaming eyes
Towards the Light
There bursts upon your sight
The Vision of the Christ
You thought would never come.
And then your life is changed.
You know the meaning now
Of peace
And love
And joy.
For these are one;
The essence of your being
The knowledge of His Presence,
The joy of coming Home at last.

And now you know
The Christ has come
And still is here.
Goodwill to all
And peace can be your part.
And He remains
In patience
Until all will seek His Face
Until one day the whole world will rejoice

And Heaven itself ring out
With peals of joy and praise.
Thank God,
Praise God,
The Christ has come.
The Christ has come at last.

1997

A Note about

Christmas

This is a different approach to the usual story of the babe in a manger in Bethlehem. I was thinking of the real meaning behind the Christmas story.

The concept of the Christ goes beyond the baby Jesus. The Christ is the perfect Son of God. Jesus realised his identification with this Vision and, as he said, what he could do we could do also. This too is our Identity. This is the Vision for us all at Christmastime.

Happiness 2

Everybody wants it
Everybody seeks it
Very few that find it.

Oh yes - you can be
Happy for a moment
Maybe two
You may find a way of living
That's "made" just for you.

But does this last?
No?
Why then do you carry on
And search the way
You have done in the past?

Is there not a better way?
A chance at least to find
That which you seek.

You think
Like all the world -
If only he or she would change
Or things, events and circumstance
Would be the way I want;
Then would I be happy.

This has not worked!
As is said, it will be all the same
If you do as you've always done
Even by another name.
But surely there's another way
And surely there is one.

The only way is God's.
And that is found within.
There is no lasting joy
In all the world
Outside of you.
But here within your mind
Is where your seeking ends
In the stillness of that Presence
-Happiness that never ends.

Mar. 2014

A Note About

Happiness 2

This, as you've no doubt observed, is a second set of verses about happiness. Happiness is a very important subject. It is what everyone wants and, in their own way everybody strives for it. But any happiness found in this world is transient and, by definition, cannot last. What lasts is Reality and that is a spiritual thing. Happiness which comes from inner peace and an awareness of one's true Identity is the only happiness than can, and does, last.

Time Heals They Say.......

Time marches on
And you, invincible
In youth, now see
Time waits for none.
You too grow old and some day
You must die.

How would you feel
If someone very close to you
Passed on;
Your beloved one
That you have loved so long
Now gone?

I too would feel as you
Bereft, alone and lonely;
Wandering down the echoing halls
With no companion by my side.
I too would feel the loss and pain,
And grief and sorrow would remain.

I too would miss the sound of voices gone
And listening ears
To catch
Some point of interest
I would share.
Now there is none to join with me
To share my nonsense or my wit
Darkness descends upon my mind
And wonders still if life is worth all this.

But....time heals they say.
How long is time,

A decade, or a year or two,
Or this month or the next?
Time heals they say,
But when?
When does grief depart
And life begin again?

Time heals, they say.
There must be reasons why.
If we but understood the reasons why
We grieve
And feel such searing loss,
This may help the healing that
Time brings.

We see ourselves as bodies
And we do not think we are alone
When bodies are around us
Keeping company
And thinking like ourselves.

We become accustomed to the face,
The gestures, manners and the grace
Of others.
Because we see ourselves as incomplete
We need assurance from another
And the gifts and blessings
They can bring to us.

And thus it is, if they are gone forever
Then we feel the greatest loss.
We are bereft
And grief sets in.

If we could only see
That bodies cannot join.
True union is with minds alone,

And minds do not need bodies
To communicate, [1]
Or join together with each other.

We look upon a dream and not reality.
For what is Real you cannot lose
Nor will it change or pass away.
And there is that real Self in each of us
That cannot die,
Or leave you cast aside, alone
And stricken with your grief.

But we need "eyes" to see
Beyond the sight of bodies;
And behold that which is really
Solid, loving, true.
For They are there;
Your Father and your Brothers
And your Home.

You cannot be alone
It is not possible.
So many loving minds
Will join with yours
If you but move beyond
Your senses
To realms of Light and Love and Joy.

Time heals they say.
This is not really true.
We but forget the past
And memory grows cold.
We no longer can recall
The days of old.
The loving face is blurred
Its actions dim
Time does not heal
But we lose trace of him.

How better far to leave this world behind
Not by dying
But by desire and willingness
To see
Reality.

This may be so, you say.
It is not easy, for I do not see
The way.

With every grief or sorrow
Loss or pain
A chance is given
To begin again.
An opportunity for something new
To happen.
A new beginning, something different
New friends to love
And share with you
A life you still must live.

The choice is always yours.
Yes, you will grieve
And time will fade the memories
Of your loss.
But there will come a time
When you decide
To grieve no more.
This will not bring him back.
And he would want you to
Press on
And not to think of things you lack.

True happiness is from within.
If you would find the way
You must begin.
And what you need is willingness to start
And Love will find its way into your heart.

Know then that you are loved,
With Everlasting Love that knows
No limits time or state.
Let go of grief
For only loss and sorrow are its train
And let your mind abide in Love
And let your life begin again.

1st. Jan. 1999

A Note about

Time Heals They Say

I wrote these verses because some said "I suppose you think that when someone close to you dies you will just go on your usual way, unlike the rest of us who will grieve in that situation, just because you believe the way you do, that death is not the end?"

It made me think.

How would I be affected if someone I loved deeply passed on?

It seemed to me that if we know that those who die reach a state of happiness and love then why do we grieve? The truth, of course, is that we are sorry for ourselves! And we have good cause to be so, because we no longer have the physical companionship of the one we loved. Because of this we feel a loneliness and lack in our lives. But does this have to be so?

So, how would I react?

I suppose one doesn't really know until that situation occurs. However, I tried to imagine how I would feel, what my reactions might be, and in pondering this I proceeded to write these verses. Doing this was a blessing to me and I trust it will be to you also as you read the thoughts that they express.

The Call

The Holy Spirit calls to you
As He calls to me.
So often we fail to hear
His Voice.
Yet He calls.
Always, never ceasing,
That you return to Him.

Here is your home
Where you belong.
There is no other place,
No other time,
No other way,
But to return to Him.

For His is the call
Of Love.
No one, in the end,
Can resist this call,
For nothing in this world
Or the universe
Beyond the sun and stars,
Will attract you like His Voice.

He calls-
Spirit to spirit
Love to love
Life to life;
And bids you come.
And now, at last,
You hear it once again.

O you can turn away
And take another path

But that goes nowhere.
Until one day, a thousand years from now,
You hear it once again
And turn to Him.

Here is your completion.
Here is all you seek.
Here is all you need.

There is nowhere else to go;
Nothing else to search for;
Nothing else to find;
Now or ever.

1998

A Note about

The Call

The Call referred to can come in any number of ways. Some hear it as a Voice, some as a very clear communication which they understand but cannot explain, some as a yearning, some as a prompting – even guilt can serve as a prompt.

But everyone hears it..
Many do not recognise it at first but it is there in each of us and, when we least expect it, it calls again.

It is always there within us and one day each of us will listen once again and answer.

Quiet Time

Quiet Time

So would I sit awhile my Lord
And listen to Your Voice,
Commune with You in quietness
And stillness.
"Be still and listen" [1]
This is what You said.
For this I know,
That You would speak with me.

And so I'm here;
For I would hear Your Words to me
For there is nothing else of value
Now or ever.
For with Your Words comes also
Oneness with You Who are
My Source
My Life,
My Being.

Always would I abide with You
For there is nowhere else to go.
My mind is badly trained
For it would take another road.

There is a part of it
Which thinks there is
Another way!
And it would look for
"Something else"'
Some other thing
Some other person
Some possession
Or experience
Some emotion

Some "high"
Excitement
Variety
Something new.

It is because I see some value in this world
My mind will not be still;
But yet wants
Something else
To stir it once again.

Because of this, it is not easy
To be still.
Mind has ideas
And tries to think
Unlike its Maker.
And so it flits about
To this thought and the next,
Always moving,
Never still,
Always wanting
Something more.

It is not easy to be still.
Our minds need training
In a greater skill.
We are too tolerant
Of wandering thoughts
That come and go
Seemingly unbidden,
Or unwanted.
This is not so.

My mind is mine.
If I would have it still
It shall be so.
My mind is mine.
I am responsible for all it does,

And I can choose to have it so.
But this takes willingness
And time,
And desire
Of one intent –
To be with You.

I have tried a thousand times
And thousands more
To find release
And happiness
And peace.
My restless mind
Seeks rest
Completion.
But never does it find the end it seeks.
Always it is "next time",
But there never is a next time
Only "NOW".

So here I stay
To meet with You.
There is no other.
For where else would I search
To find the only thing I seek
Or want.
Here it is!
Now!
For in Your Presence
There is peace and joy.
Here stillness is
And here I rest at last.

2002

[1]   W-pl.106.7:5

A Note about

Quiet Time

Because, as Jesus said, "The Kingdom of God is within you" it is necessary to go within to find it. Makes sense?

To do this we need our minds to be still. Our minds are a bit like the ocean; lots of activity, wind and noise on the surface but deep down below all is still.

Deep within the stillness of our mind is where we hear the Voice that would speak with us.

The seers down through the ages have all given the same encouragement –

"Only be still and listen"

Epilogue

We walk together you and me, along the road that leads to Him.
We cannot go back, for now we know that happiness does not lie there
So we press on knowing that from Him we cannot wander for there is no
state, no place where He is not.

"Remember always you cannot be anywhere except in the mind of God" [1]

"Wake up to understand that you have always been the expression of God,
that you have always lived in a state of absolute harmony. Do not attempt to
involve your intellect in an understanding of how something could appear
to be so real and yet be called by me merely a dream. There will be no
understanding for it. And do not resist it, do not try to get out of it, or think
that by dying you will go from one plane to another.

There is no place for you to go. You are now at Home. You have always been
at Home and it will only be when you allow that recognition to dawn upon
your mind that you will see it being so. You will see the glory of God that has
always been around you. You will see the state of Love that you have always
been in. But you will not see it if you resist it or try to make it so. Just give
up knowing that it is not so.
There is nothing else to do."

- Jesus [2]

May the blessing of God rest upon you
May His peace abide with you
May His Presence illuminate your heart
Now and forever more.
- Sufi Blessing

[1]   T -9.VIII.5:3
[2]   Extract from:
       Dialogue on Awakening - P250
       Tom & Linda Carpenter
       The Carpenter Press
       P.O. Box 3437
       Princeville, Hawaii 96722